NEW LIGHT ON 1776 AND ALL THAT

NEW LIGHT ON 1776 AND ALL THAT

 Richard Bissell

Illustrations by Ron Carreiro

LITTLE, BROWN AND COMPANY
BOSTON - TORONTO

FIRST EDITION

T 10/75

LIBRARY OF CONGRESS CATALOGING IN PUBLICATION DATA

Bissell, Richard Pike.
1776 and all that. Boston, Little, Brown and Company, 1975.

174 p.
19 cm.

1. United States—History—Revolution, 1775–1783—Humor, caricatures, etc. I. Title.
E298.B57   973.3′02′07   75-19206
ISBN 0-316-09670-9

E
298
B57

Designed by Susan Windheim

*Published simultaneously in Canada
by Little, Brown & Company (Canada) Limited*

PRINTED IN THE UNITED STATES OF AMERICA

Contents

Notice!

Two score and five years ago, in March 1930 to be specific, English speaking peoples as well as many Americans began to laugh at a slim volume, a parody of English history, called 1066 AND ALL THAT. Written by two funny fellows down from Oxford (or is it up?), the book sold for $1.75 U.S.A. on a money back guarantee that it contained "one hundred and three good things, five bad kings, and two genuine dates." The World has been chuckling over it ever since except for a few time-outs to produce some new history such as wars, abdications, the mini-skirt, et cetera.

In presenting an historical work of the present kind the greatest demand on an author is not the dogged, meticulous research but the seeking out of an answer to the question "Where can I steal a good title?"

After fasting, retreat, and transcontinental meditation I have rejected as unsuitable the following titles: *War and Peace, Advise and Consent, Summer and Smoke,* and *Penrod and Sam.*

Ultimately, in an altruistic desire to extend "hands across the sea," I have decided to promote friendship and brotherhood by borrowing three quarters of Messrs. W. C. Sellar and R. J. Yeatman's title.

So it's Rule Britannia and long live Betsy Ross! God save the Queen and bless Mr. President! For England never shall be slave but Yankee Doodle always macaroni. Homage to apple pie and the patriotic hot dog and long live overcooked brussels sprouts!

All is forgiven, George, and you too, Cornwallis, you fathead.

R. B.

NEW LIGHT ON
1776
AND ALL THAT

☞ **ONE** ☜

PREPOSTEROUS!
     Upstarts! Pipsqueaks! Codfish eaters! Hicks!
Wamblers! Noddles! Oafs!

Childish Colonials all — how did we do it? How did
we knock off King George's crown, the actual crown
first worn in 1662 by Charles II ("Old Rowley")? His
crown which contains to this day rosettes and circlets
of rubies and diamonds, four crosses-patés and four
fleur-de-lys adorned with diamonds, with two complete arches of gem-encrusted gold surmounted by a
mound of gold and a richly jewelled cross?

That kind of regal headgear is hard to come by. Yet
seventy Colonial rubes and a drummer boy in the puny
pathetic village of Lexington, Massachusetts, sent it
tumbling across the palace parquetry to crash against
the fire tongs. Taking out the crimps and resetting
various priceless gems cost the Treasury 34 pounds,
8 sovereigns, 6 guineas, 4 crowns, 5 half-crowns, 12

shillings, 6 sixpennys, 5 pennys, 32 ha'pennys, 254 farthings, and 12 tweedlies (a very small coin).

France and Spain couldn't do it. How could a passel of rustics with their toes sticking out of holes in their shoes pull it off?

What was the matter with the King's troops when they stepped on our unsophisticated soil? Why did they behave so like boobies? Why did that great royal warrior Lord Howe spend the winter of 1777–1778 playing Winkum and Postoffice in Philadelphia? Why didn't he go 20 miles out to Valley Forge and wipe the slate? He could of been back in town in time for the matinee.

There were only 2.5 million people here, stretched from Passamaquoddy to Key Biscayne, and west to the Alleghenies and the Ohio River Valley where the human beings resembled trained bears. The population was 90% hayseeds, who chewed on straws while their wives improved their time in preparing for the next Arts and Crafts Show by spinning, weaving, doing cross stitch, fabricating dreary "samplers" and making up folklore. The production of manufactured goods was pathetic. How could this bunch of counter-culture candlemakers expect to fight a war with the dragon of St. George which would require thousands upon thousands of bullets, Band-Aids, and bottle openers?

Britain was the greatest power on earth and very scary. She had all the ships and all the shoes and sealing wax and 9 million people. In far off places the sun

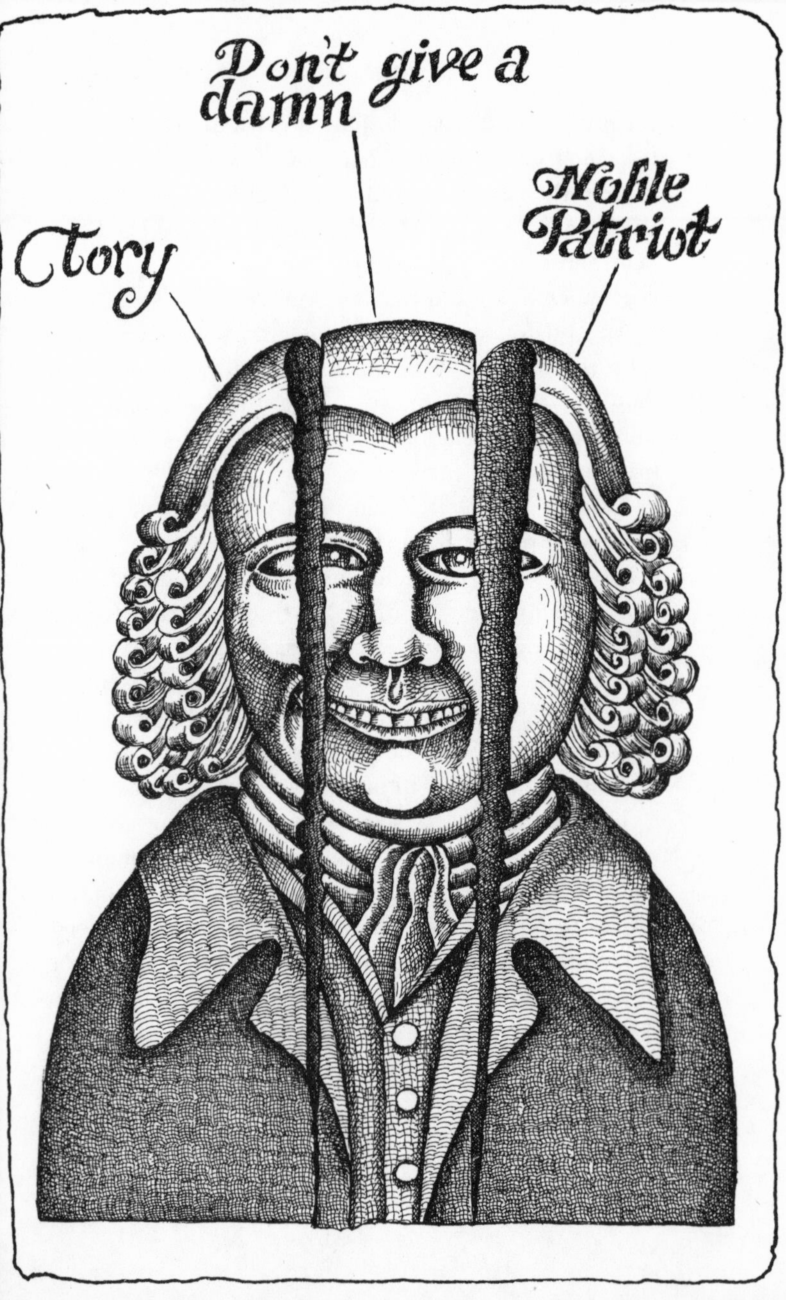
Don't give a damn
Tory
Noble Patriot

usually set on Britons sloshing down Pimms Cup. And by 1769 Captain James Cook had visited Tahiti, where he left the beach littered with Gordon's gin bottles. Britain also had formidable apparatus such as Dr. Samuel Johnson, the most terrifying and scrofulous lexicographer the world has ever known.

And on top of it all, the colonists themselves were split three ways. One third were Tories, one third didn't give a damn one way or tother, and only one third of the population were Noble Patriots breathing fire and spitting buck shot.

Teacher doesn't tell the Fifth Grade about it but there was plenty of fistfights and eye gouging right inside the colonial regiments. Virginians hated Bay Staters, Nutmeggers loathed North Carolinians, Rhode Islanders sneered at Vermonters, Pennsylvanians despised New Hampshiremen, and Everybody spit on New Yorkers. John Adams and the New England fire-eaters never did like George Washington — he was one of those high tone Virginians.

The colonial forces spent most of the war years in retreating. The colonial armies had the full military clout of thirteen Mexican policemen arguing politics on a streetcorner in Vera Cruz. When they stopped retreating and engaged in battle they usually got slugged. The number of battles lost to the British is very depressing.

After getting crumped at Hobkirk's Hill in April

of 1781, General Greene stated: "We fight, get beat, rise, and fight again."

This inelegant mulishness is the reason why today we drive on the right side of the road, and don't eat with our fork in the left hand and upside down. With mashed potatoes smeared on top of the forkful of meat (overcooked.)

But it also so happened that our boys won a few Saturday afternoon upsets and two or three of the Big Ones that count.

You might say some of these were not big league battles but to the boys who didn't eat supper that night and who didn't go home they were battles.

As you can see it was often a long time between wins for the foes of St. George.

The War, in fact, was 1½ years old and England had had two general transport strikes, three general post-office strikes, as well as crippling strikes in digestive biscuits, cricket stumps, and trivets, before the Continentals could claim a victory in the field. It was G. Washington's surprise attack on Trenton, on Christmas night of 1776. This victory proved to the British that it is a very poor idea to hire a General who will get loaded on Christmas day when G. Washington is in the neighborhood.

Then after our lads with the help of crazy-o Benedict Arnold had defused Gentleman Johnny Burgoyne at Saratoga in October '77, it was three painful years

AMERICAN REVOLUTION
1775–1782
BATTLES, SIEGES, SKIRMISHES, ETC.

FINAL SCORE

WE	THEY
	1775
	Bunker Hill
	Falmouth
	Quebec
	1776
Siege of Boston	The Cedars
Moores Creek Bridge	Trois Rivières
Fort Sullivan	Valcour Island
Trenton	Long Island
	Kips Bay
	White Plains
	Fort Washington
	Fort Lee
	1777
Princeton	Danbury
Fort Stanwix	Metuchen
Bennington	Ticonderoga
Saratoga	Hubbardton
	Fort Ann

FINAL SCORE (Cont.)

WE   THEY

Oriskany
Brandywine
Paoli
Philadelphia
Germantown
Fort Mifflin
White Marsh

1778

Kaskaskia   Wyoming
Quaker Hill
Cherry Valley
Savannah

1779

Vincennes   Penobscot Expedition
Stony Point   Siege of Savannah
Paulus Hook
Kettle Creek

1780

Hanging Rock   Young's House
Kings Mountain   Siege of Charleston
Moncks Corner
Waxhaws
Camden
Fishing Creek

FINAL SCORE (Cont.)

WE   THEY

1781

WE	THEY
The Cowpens	Guilford Court House
Glorious YORKTOWN	Hobkirks Hill
	Ninety Six
	Cane Creek
	Eutaw Springs

Draws

1775	Lexington-Concord
1778	Monmouth

until they could toss their funny tri corner hats in the air again, cry "huzza," and issue other quaint period outcries of exultation over a genuine First Class Victory. It was a decidedly downish three years which saw not only disaster at Brandywine and Germantown, calamity at Charleston, and humiliation at Camden, but actual mutinies in the armies under G. Washington. (It seems these troops wanted something to eat besides turnips and they thought it would be nice to get six months of their back pay so they could buy some rum and get soused like everybody else.)

Valley Forge also fell into this period and has always been a godsend to patriotic poets, tunesmiths and scripters of elementary school dramas.

It was mighty unpleasant there and they kept running out of Sterno. One feels that a more intelligent leadership would have marched south and wintered at someplace more like Coral Gables or Daytona Beach. New Jersey was just as infinitely depressing in colonial days as it is now, and Washington's winter quarters at Morristown provided tortures as bad as Valley Forge; but the Forge purloined the headlines on bloody footprints in the snow and Morristown has, like our 37½th President, never gotten a square deal from the press publicitywise.

It wasn't until October of 1780, at a time when the glorious autumnal foliage of the Carolinas was receiving its annual editorial comment in the Charlotte and Gastonia papers, that victory came again to the patriot cause and it was as sweet as Catawba Valley apple squeezings. It was at Kings Mountain, North Carolina, that Isaac Shelby and Richard Campbell with their Carolina and Virginia sharpshooters blasted Major Patrick Ferguson off the rock, together with his 1100 crack Tory riflemen.

This felicitous issue was followed in four months by another grand slam, at the Cowpens, over that bloody limey bastard, cold-steel Banastre Tarleton, who was soundly thumped this time and chased 18 miles through the woods instead of vice versa. But we were not home free yet by a long shot of cannister — ahead lay further humiliation, woe at Eutaw Springs, and more hamburger at Guilford Court House.

Until that jocund occasion when Charles, Earl Cornwallis, from the playing fields of Eton, husband to witty, willowy and charming Jemima Tullikens, wandered out to Yorktown-sur-Mer and decided it would be a nice place to camp. He was a bum picker of camp sites and it was all so Typical of this whole strange war.

The Britons are a curious race indeed, and for losing the colonies and General Motors forever, Lord Charles Cornwallis Cornwallis was rewarded with a Marquessate, Governor Generalship of India, became Master General of the Ordnance with Cabinet Rank, and was made Viceroy of Ireland.

But as a dub Cornwallis was not alone.

Let's face it, fellow Amurricans, the generalship on both sides in the glorious American Revolution was Katzenjammer stuff. It was "Mutt and Jeff at the Front" or "Abbott and Costello Meet the Redcoats."

The British at home thought that George Washington as a general was a dodo. When it became apparent that their own sleepy General Howe couldn't beat Washington they came to the conclusion they were both dodos.

A crusty British major-general with the gout and a purple nose wrote in 1778: "In short, I am of the opinion that any other General in the world than General Howe would have beaten General Washington; and any other General in the world than George Washington would have beaten General Howe."

But long before the hot lead began to fly in 1775 Americans already had an opinion on King George's regal redcoats. They had had one ever since July, 1755, when that musical-comedy military dunce, General Edward Braddock, late of the Coldstream Guards, marched his army in close order formation into the charnel house of the forest primeval before Fort Duquesne on the Monongahela.

"This whole transaction," Benjamin Franklin remarked of the event years later at a stove jobbers' convention in Altoona, "gave us Americans the first suspicion that our exalted ideas of the prowess of British regulars had not been well founded."

But every time we won a battle it was always to the complete amazement of the English and European warriors on the field, and of King George, Parliament, and the folks in Stoke Poges, Lyme Regis, and Tarfington-on-Thames, who not only were using the upside-down fork in the left hand but were referring to stagecoach "shed-yules."

And for generations American schoolboys in the 4th and 5th grades have been quitting school and going to work at the box factory to escape hearing any more about Bunker Hill and the good ole Townshend Acts (which believe me will not be mentioned again).

In the words of Dr. Samuel Johnson:

"Sir, your War is like a one-legged cordwainer. Sir, your Battles are desipient gullery in a jiggery-pokery of foolsprock. Sir, please to pay the check."

Now I Lay Me...

To Brookfield. Lodged with Mrs. Baldwin and you may guess for ye rest.

COLONEL JEDUTHAN BALDWIN,
enroute home from the Battle
of Germantown.

☞ **TWO** ☜

IT DIDN'T JUST HAPPEN all at once.

The colonies all up and down the coast and the full length of the Appalachian chain had been blowing their tops at frequent intervals for years. They fretted and made noises. For one thing they didn't like "tyranny." Now your average European, African, or Oriental was mighty uncomfortable if there wasn't any tyranny on hand because he was used to it. But not these Colonials, who were already turning into Americans who don't take no sass off nobody. The Tories of course didn't mind tyranny. The English rather like it only today they are getting it from the labor unions instead of the government.

The anti-tyranny element had also discovered early on that if thirteen little guys ganged up they had a better chance against Luke the Town Bully than by kicking him in the shins separately.

The colonies had held off the Indians (sorry about

that, Marlon) and they had crunched French power on their borders into little bitty *morceaux*. They had done this for the glory of the British Crown and their own preservation, usually without much help or any particular interest or gratitude from the folks back in Piccadilly or the fans eating bubble and squeak in the pubs of Hampstead Heath. For their reward they got condescension, sneers, rude remarks, the Stamp Act, taxes, port closings, and an ignorant soldiery quartered upon them as uninvited house guests.

The French and Indian war, a bestial, bloody, barbaric, and slow affair, had left them a bit cocky. They had looked good in the preliminaries and their promoters, Sam and John Adams, Hancock, T. Jefferson, et al., just thought they might be able to handle the big one.

If King George the Third and his ministers hadn't been such a bunch of bozos they would have realized that they had knocked down the hornet's nest but they didn't, for they were a bunch of bozos from Bozoland.

George's grandfather, George Two, whom he succeeded, had been as weird a monarch as ever ruled. His father, Frederick, Prince of Wales, was also absurd. George wasn't as whacky as the old gent but he was a buck and if he ever took any good advice in regard to the Colonies it's not in the record book.

England as a result of constant wars was about busted financially at this time in point. So to get up some easy money to fix the roof at Hampton Court and provide more plum duff for the British fleet, George and his parliament proceeded to tax the colonies.

They led right into the hands of "Sorehead Sam" Adams of Boston and his buddies, and irritable citizens all the way down the coast. A recent tenant of the ovoid room in Washington would call these soreheads and agitators "irresponsible liberals" and possibly even "bums," but they have come down in history as Patriots, to be used frequently in campaign speeches.

It was the first time an English king had attempted to lay taxes on his subjects except by their own representatives since the time of King John nearly 600 years before. (John was the son of Henry II and Eleanor of Aquitaine. George was the son of Frederick, Prince of Wales, who had been arrested for nutty behavior by his own father and thrown out of St. James's, and Augusta, a German princess of Saxe-Gotha who talked English with a komical Kissinger accent. Her only claim to fame is that when her son ascended the Britannic throne she said, "Be King, George; be King." He followed this motherly advice with the usual results.)

The effect of the Stamp Act of 1765 could have been predicted by the stupidest pot-boy in Newburyport or Coinjock, S.C. While two-thirds of the population locked their doors and tried to act natural, the mutineers in Boston, New York and other principal points began to march and howl. Ben Franklin wrote from England: "The Sun of Liberty is set . . ."

A mob of unattractive people plundered the government storehouse in Boston and wrecked Lieutenant Governor Hutchinson's house. Out in Cambridge the Harvard lads rushed over to the Square and had a riot, the first they had staged in almost two weeks. When the king's stamp salesmen tried to sell their wares they were roughed up and made to feel unwanted. Nobody bought the stamps, which were required on all newspapers, legal documents, etc. Business closed down. Counting houses shuttered and quill pushers went rowing with Miss Tewksbury.

George finally got the message and the Stamp Act was repealed in 1766, but he was mightily peeved at Boston, which he considered the "most impudent and unruly city" in his realm. And two years later he sent troops to Boston. The people said to hell with that and refused to quarter them or furnish barracks so the lobsterbacks camped on Boston Common and in Faneuil Hall. There was also a fleet of eight ominous men-of-war parked in Boston harbor.

The street mobs and gawks spent their entire spare time in baiting the redcoats, throwing snowballs at them on every occasion and provoking them into fistfights. The city for all its patrician airs had a large floating population of rowdies, hooligans and knaves which it has to this day. These crude members of the unwashed acted in mobs and enjoyed throwing bricks through windows, busting property and serving out bloody noses all around. The troops themselves acted haughty and arrogant instead of protective ("damn bloody cod-eating Bostoners").

The Beantown stage was now set and lighted for a first class incident. "Sorehead Sam" Adams continued to fuss and fume, and smoke was often seen coming out of his ears. Unpleasant confrontations between citizens, toughs and bullyboys and the British troops continued. Adams egged on the "inhabitants of the lower classes" and warned the towns round about that something was going to happen, possibly on March fifth. Adams was looking for some good martyrs. Well, *one* would do, but if the redcoats could be tormented to the point of firing on a mob there might be more. So much the better for Liberty.

On the fifth of March 1770 Boston was under a foot of snow. It was cold at first but later it began to warm up, as it always does. Boston's winter specialty is slush.

In the afternoon a British soldier, thinking to make a little money on the side, for their pay was pathetic, went to Gray's ropewalks, on Hutchinson Street, now Pearl Street, to see if there was any part-time work. He confronted a journeyman there named Sam Gray, no relation to the management.

"So you want work, do you?" said Sam.

"Yes, I want to work," replied the redcoat.

"Good. You can clean my shithouse," replied Sam, and the fight was on.

This exchange of snappy dialogue, which resulted later that night in the "Boston Massacre," although

authentic, does not appear in any school textbooks that I know of.

In the scrimmage that resulted Sam Gray clobbered the soldier, who ran back to barracks for reinforcements. A full scale melee then took place in which either the King's men were beaten to a fare-thee-well or the ropemakers, depending on which sources you consult. At any rate the brawl was broken up and the soldiers retired in a bad frame of mind. This bloody broil left the whole town agog, and by nightfall the narrow streets were filled with roaming groups of rude soldiers and cursing American rabble.

About eight P.M. an assemblage of our forefathers was congregated in front of the custom-house. John Adams described this group as consisting of "saucy boys, negroes, mulattos, Irish teagues, and outlandish Jack tars." There were plenty of Bostonians in other categories there also and they were having a grand time badgering the lone sentry, whose name was Montgomery, casting doubts on his ancestry, and pelting him with the usual snowballs, oyster shells, hunks of coal, ripe codfish and dead cats. Montgomery got tired of this and called for help from the barracks. Captain Preston came to his aid with eight armed men.

The mob dared them to fire and Isaac Greenwood hollered "Fire away, you damned lobster backs." They complied and five citizens were killed, including an enormous mulatto from Framingham called Crispus Attucks.

That was the "Boston Massacre," America's first and most dearly beloved atrocity.

Governor Hutchinson rushed to the scene, sore at both sides. He roared at the crowd from the balcony of the State House that justice would be done.

Before dawn Captain Preston and the eight imprudent marksmen were under arrest for murder.

To prove to King George that such a thing as order and justice existed in the crude swamps of North America, the culprits were defended in a court of law by two noted men of the popular movement, John Adams and Josiah Quincy. Captain Preston and six of his men were acquitted. The other two were charged with manslaughter. They claimed benefit of clergy and were branded on the hand and dismissed.

Sam Gray, who had touched things off by offering employment with regard to his sanitary facilities, was one of the men killed in the massacre, and killed by a notorious ruffian and thief in the soldiery named, of all things, Kilroy. Not for 172 years was the name Kilroy to appear again in our military history, creating world-wide ennui.

Beautiful.

Sam Adams had five martyrs and worked them overtime.

Crispus Attucks the mulatto divided up into ⅓ black martyr, ⅓ Indian martyr, and ⅓ white martyr. A bonanza.

For many many years the Anniversary of the "Boston Massacre" was celebrated with inflamed passions, dense clouds of hot air, no mail service and no garbage collections. I expect it will be revived soon by Act of Congress, as school children and gov't employees now only have two national holidays per week and one half-holiday in March in memory of Roy C. Teagarden, inventor of the parking meter.

Shortly after these events the colonists staged the First and Second Continental Congresses. Ostensibly to unite in opposition to the crown and publish saucy proclamations, the real purpose was to drive future school children out of their minds trying to figure out which Continental Congress was which, and why Patrick Henry said it.

It seemed rash.

Everybody appeared to be slightly crazy. That's the only part perfectly clear to the 5th Grade.

Because everybody still is.

All Right, Boys, Move Her West about 500 Feet

The Boston Massacre site is being moved. A cobblestone marker, noting the March 5, 1770, skirmish in which five persons were killed by British troops, is being moved 500 feet west for what are called 'safety reasons.' The traffic congestion is expected to be less at the new site near the corner of State and Congress Street.

Preservation News
November, 1972

THREE

RIGHT TODAY, this minute, there is a test tube on display at the Old North Church in Boston, full of a deplorably murky brown liquid. It is tea made from some leftover tea leaves brought home from the Boston Tea Party. I wish I had some and I could sell it to the University of Texas. They will buy anything. And I could retire and leave New England, which has very dreary winters.

My ancestor Joseph Bissell had a pew in the Old North Church but he was probably out at the Brookline Country Club playing draw poker that night and no historic tea leaves have descended to me.

Of all the crazy hooligan stunts pulled off by the colonies against England, the Boston Tea Party was the wildest.

The first ship to arrive in Boston with the detestable tea was the *Dartmouth*. The owner's name was Rotch and he was warned not to unload her or else. Paul

Revere and twenty-five other armed patriots stood by all night on the wharf.

Presently two more ships appeared at Griffin's Wharf, the *Beaver* and the *Eleanor*, loaded with 342 chests of offensive Bohea.

Rampageous protest meetings were held. "Sorehead Sam" Adams was in the thick of it. The rabble was delirious with joy. Schoolmasters closed up shop and took the lads to see the fun. It was the origin of the educational "field trip," carried on to this day, meaning no school and lots of pushing.

On December 16th 1773 a typical frantic Bostonian mob of 7000 mixed wahoos was jammed into Old South Church and packed in the streets outside. Speechifiers spewed forth brimstone, red hot bolts and chain shot.

"Send them ships back to Blighty" was the general theme. "Get that there tea out of here."

Just imagine such a fuss about tea.

Principle, my boy, principle, not tea.

Governor Hutchinson had prudently retired to Milton for the day. Not the Academy, the town, where he pulled down the shades and had several hot buttered rums.

Mr. Rotch was sent out to Milton to get permission for clearance papers to send the ticklish tea back to London river.

Hutch said no, Rotch, he couldn't do that, it was illegal.

By the time Rotch had covered the seven miles back to the meeting it was quarter to six and dark.

When Rotch announced to the overheated assemblage that the Governor had refused to turn loose the ships, "Sorehead Sam" got up and hollered.

"This meeting can do nothing more to save the country!!"

This was the tipoff line and was greeted by war whoops and such unlikely gems of dialogue as: "Boston harbor a tea-pot tonight!"

What happened next on the program and occupied a good part of the night is the only thing about the American Revolution that any of the boys down at the Elks Club can remember except George and the cherry tree.

It is part of our American Heritage — which also includes Franklin Pierce, Peaches Browning, Mrs. John Dean and the McNary-Haugen Farm Bill.

There was nothing very secret about the Tea Party. A crowd of thousands watched. The ship was at the wharf and they saw the hatches opened and the tea chests hoisted out, broken and tossed into the bay. Dramatically it was somewhat of a bust since the tide was low and the tea landed in the mud. But when the tide rose a windrow of oolong extended clear to Dorchester.

"I never worked harder in my life," Joshua Wyeth, then age fifteen, said afterwards.

Why didn't the British squadron, anchored less than

a quarter of a mile away, interrupt the affair? Because Admiral Montague watched the entire soiree from a Tory friend's house right there on Griffin's Wharf.

When it was all over he stuck his head out the window and remarked:

"Well boys, you have had a fine, pleasant evening for your Indian caper — haven't you? But mind, you have got to pay the fiddler yet."

The tea-snatchers replied with catcalls and some dialogue even more improbable than that of Admiral Montague.

When George Robert Twelves Hewes returned home and told his wife Sally that he had spent the night dumping tea into Boston harbor, she filled in for Blondie Bumstead and said, "Well George did you bring me a lot of it?"

"You are just like your mother," he replied, "more of a tea-drinker than a Whig."

"How did my mother get into the conversation?" she said, and they both went to bed mad.

Thomas Melville got home and took off his shoes and found them full of tea and put it in a glass bottle. Maybe that's the tea I saw at the Old North Church.

Anyway I wish I had some. I would sell it to the University of Texas. They'll buy anything.

John and Sam and Some Other Bostonians

John Adams (Harvard 1755) was dumpy, florid, vain and blunt. Ben Franklin said he was honest, a great man, and "sometimes positively mad." He was afflicted with inborn contentiousness. He didn't like Ben Franklin, George Washington, or in fact hardly anybody. He was sore at Jefferson most of the time and thought that he should have written the Declaration of Independence instead of Thomas. He broke with Hamilton. He was loaded with personality, most of it rotten. How he ever got elected President is a mystery. When he was defeated by Jefferson for a second term he was so exasperated that he packed up and went home mad to Quincy without waiting for the inauguration.

Samuel Adams, also dumpy (Harvard 1740), was a second cousin to John and 13 years older. He was a chronic bankrupt in business. Naturally he was not fond of taxes and blamed all his tough luck on the regime. He was a nonstop talker and writer of sizzling revolutionary polemics. He was a dusty man with a quavery voice constantly heard on street corners, in taverns and in Faneuil Hall. He was indignant, impassioned, incensed and outraged, and never shut up about it. He was the first American to get up in a public assembly and declare for absolute independence. As an agitator he makes Vladimir Ilitch and Trotsky look like pikers.

After the Revolution a grateful citizenry elected him governor of the State of Massachusetts. It was the only job he ever held without going bust.

John Hancock (Harvard 1754) inherited his Uncle's mercantile business in Boston and a large fortune at the age of twenty-seven. In fact one of the biggest piles in New England, £50,000 sterling. However, he managed to blow most of it. He was stuck on himself and had some fairly absurd personal characteristics.

In 1768 he was trying to smuggle a cargo of Madeira wine from one of his ships, the sloop *Liberty*. The customs lads caught him and confiscated the ship. This turned him against the Crown — for next to himself, he was fondest of his money. Sam Adams latched onto him at this point.

He was born and died at Quincy, Mass., pronounced Quinzy.

Dr. Joseph Warren (Harvard 1759) a blube and a leader of the popular party in Boston. Drafted the "Suffolk Resolves," a nose-thumber pointed toward the Thames. Handsome, resolute, a man for all seasons, still very big in the hearts of Bostonians.

Dr. Warren volunteered at the Battle of Bunker Hill and was killed by a British officer who recognized him, grabbed a gun from a private, and shot him dead at close quarters.

As we see, all the above partisans of liberty and fomentors of rebellion were Harvard men. If they had been Yale men they would have all gone down to Wall Street to sell bonds and there would have been no American Revolution.

☞ **FOUR** ☜

KING GEORGE OF ENGLAND was not in a very good humour when he read in the morning papers about the Boston Tea Party. He called in Lord North and said, "North old bean, bear down on those Boston smart-alecks."

So North gave the sign to Parliament and they passed a bill closing the entire port of Boston to all commercial transactions whatever. Governor Hutchinson was then relieved (in more ways than one) and General Gage was sent up from New York to act as military governor and enforce the Port Bill.

Boston went into bankruptcy. Wharves were empty, counting houses gloomy, quill-drivers out of work, and Indian pudding became scarce. Town meetings were abolished and all civic power was vested in the governor and his toadies. Sam Adams had a mild case of apoplexy and John Hancock went on Gelusil.

All Americans were distraught and peevish even

down in the southern colonies, where strife had become rife against the rapacity and general orneriness of the royal governors. Massachusetts invited all the other colonies to meet in Philadelphia in September 1774, forgetting that Sundays in Philadelphia are deadly and night life is nonexistent.

This was the FIRST CONTINENTAL CONGRESS, children, and everybody came except Georgia, who had gone fishing. They called it the *First Continental Congress* to throw King George off the scent and spread confusion in Hyde Park. It was actually the Third Colonial Congress, the First having been held at Albany in 1754, and the Second at New York in 1765 to discuss Paving Contracts, Welfare Frauds, and Air Pollution.

In all its proceedings at Philadelphia, the Congress kept cool — displaying noble traits of decorum, firmness, moderation and even loyalty to St. George. Bookbinder's Restaurant did a land office business in stuffed crabs and everybody went home feeling righteous.

Great Britain did not respond.

Massachusetts began to prepare for war. Companies of militia were formed in every town. And even in several qualified hamlets. Veterans of the French and Indian wars stopped boring their friends with reminiscences of Fort Necessity and began to drill the yokels on village commons. These companies were called Minute-men, because theoretically it only took them one minute to get their pants on and grab their muskets. Later on a cynic in the Pennsylvania line said it was because they only fought for a minute before leaving for home.

Gunpowder and firearms were manufactured and stored. Every colonial household soon had as many guns laying around as the well appointed home of 1975.

Things got pretty warm for Sam Adams and John Hancock. They went out to visit the folks in Lexington for awhile.

One of the principal patriot munitions dumps was at Concord, six miles beyond Lexington.

General Gage decided to send a force out there to Concord to mess up the military stores. He had a "most-wanted crook" order out on Adams and Hancock and thought he might pick them up on the same trip. Later, on June 1, when Gage put out a feeler in the way of a proclamation of pardon to all rebels who would mend their ways, he made a special exception of Sam Adams and Hancock, saying that their offenses were "of too flagitious a nature to admit of any other consideration than that of condign punishment."

The redcoats should of stood at home. Eight hundred of them trudged out to Lexington in the middle of the night and arrived in the morning of April 19, 1775, at Lexington Common where they shot and killed eight militiamen. They proceeded to Concord, but found that the rural bumpkins had removed most of the explosives and hardware. They destroyed 60 barrels of flour, 3 cannon, and some wooden spoons. Who decided wooden spoons were a threat to His Majesty's Empire remains unclear. Then they threw 500 lbs of cannon balls into the pond.

At the rustic bridge, today bedecked with Baby Ruth and Wrigley's gum wrappers, an unknown patriot fired at the redcoats — the Shot Heard Round the World. Actually it probably was not even heard over at Waltham. That started the war right there.

The British then returned to Boston, being sniped at the entire way, a particularly irritating and non-cricket type of warfare to regular troops.

They lost 273 men on the way back to Boston and voted the expedition a washout.

What about Paul Revere?

The Smithsonian Institution, which cannot tell a lie, says that:

Paul was not in Charlestown but in Boston when the lanterns were raised in the Old North Church.

Paul came by a different road than the one the British were taking.

Paul did not holler "The British are coming!" He didn't holler anything.

The purpose of his trip was to tell Adams and Hancock to make themselves scarce.

On arrival in Lexington he sat down and had a midnight snack consisting of cold codfish balls and studgy beans.

What was ace patriot Hancock doing that lovely spring night? Was he writing a defiant manifesto or cataloguing royal flagitiousness? No, he was sitting up with beautiful Miss Dorothy Quincy and having a lovers' spat.

In Lincoln, Mass., the only patriot found awake was Nathaniel Baker, who was "holding hands with a fair maid named Elizabeth Taylor."

How come Paul Revere ran into Dr. Samuel Prescott on the way from Lexington to Concord? Was he out helping to rouse "every Middlesex village and farm?" Not so. He was going home from a late date with his girl friend, Miss Mulliken.

Six British officers seized Revere shortly afterwards, laid a gun to his noggin and told him to start talking. Sad to relate, Longfellow's pride and joy sang like a canary bird.

After pumping him dry, the king's men turned him loose but kept his horse, which belonged to Deacon John Larkin of Charlestown and was out on loan. The deacon never got his horse back. The horse's name was Brown Betty.

The news of the Rebel vs. Crown shootout spread like the itch (*Sarcoptes scabiei*), and from all over New England rabid patriots stampeded to Boston. By the end of the month of April, 1775, the British were bottled up in Boston by a primitive "army" of 20,000 colonials in a fortified line extending from Roxbury to the Mystic river.

The last survivor of the battles of Lexington and Concord was Jonathan Harrington, who played the

fife for the Minute-men on the morning of the battle. He died in March, 1854, at the age of 95.

Henry Wadsworth Longfellow, who had most of it wrong, died in March, 1882.

Military Stores Accumulated by the Patriot Cause Long Before the Shot Heard Round the World

In 1774 the Massachusetts Provincial Congress voted the sum of £15,627 sterling for the purchase of the following military apparatus and warlike combustibles:

    20 fieldpieces (cannon)
    4 mortars (fat cannon)
    20 tons of grape and round shot (cannonballs)
    10 tons of bombshells (exploding cannonballs)
    5 tons of bullets
    1000 barrels of powder
    5000 muskets and bayonets
    75,000 flints
    350 spades and pickaxes
    1000 wooden messbowls

Several hundred barrels of pork, flour, dried
peas and rice.

In December of '74 four hundred patriots overpow-
ered the British garrison at Fort William and Mary in
Portsmouth, N. H., and stole 97 barrels of powder,
1500 muskets, and several artillery pieces.

Forty-four cannons were stolen from Fort Island in
Rhode Island and transported to Providence "to pre-
vent their falling into the hands of the King."

☞ **FIVE** ☜

TWO WEEKS BEFORE the Battle of Bunker Hill a Boston Tory wrote to his brother in England and I quote in part:

"Good God! Do Thou avert the impending calamity that threatens this former happy land, and turn the hearts of those deluded wretches from the power of sin and Satan to Thy unerring precepts, and then, and then only, shall we be once more a happy people favoured of Heaven . . .

"O tempora! O mores! Yrs. as usual.

"PETER OLIVER JNR."

God must have an awful time trying to decide whose side he is on. I wouldn't want that kind of work.

In this case the Almighty split the honors. He gave England and St. George the victory but awarded the glory to the people's army of the Rebellion.

All in all it was a shocking affair, as human conflicts are likely to be. "War is hell," General William Tecumseh Sherman said later on, and hell is Beelzebub's department.

This battle was fought by bumbling amateurs on one side, facing professionals of the highest possible cachet on the other, and it was carried out with dementia in both quarters.

It was marked on the British side with stupidity, on the American side by stupidity, ineptitude, insubordination, desertion, panic, rotten planning, cowardice, and sore feet from running away from the fight. Both contestants also displayed many examples of bravery, the bravest, as is customary, ending up Dead.

Doctor Jeremy Belknap, a historian, trudged over the messy battlefield after the smoke had cleared and the gore had been swept up and decided that it had been "a most hazardous and imprudent affair on both sides."

The Americans placed themselves in a perilously advanced position with nearly impossible means of retreat. The British could have cut them off in the rear with ten men carrying broomsticks but chose instead a terrible and reckless frontal assault.

More Katzenjammer stuff. Von Moltke would have plucked out his beard and jumped into the frog pond. Von Mackensen would have cashiered Gage, Burgoyne, Clinton, Howe, Ward, Stark, Prescott, Putnam, stripped epaulets wholesale from both sets of contenders and made the drummer boys go to bed without any jujubes.

Our sovereign — he was still our sovereign, since we had not yet resigned as subjects aud turned in our keys to the washroom — sent three British Generals straight from the casting office of J. Arthur Rank productions to the stewpot of dissent called Boston, named for Boston town in Lincolnshire. They arrived on the 25th of May in the *Cerberus*. Their names were Howe, Clinton and Burgoyne. They were dismayed to discover that Boston was really and truly surrounded by the patriotic horde and that the supply of brussels sprouts from farms in Waban, Woburn, Wellesley, Waltham, Watertown, Winthrop, Westwood, Weymouth, Wayland, Winchester, Wakefield, Walpole and even Wrentham had been completely cut off.

"We will soon make elbow room," said General Burgoyne. This simple remark was quoted far and wide by the Tories as a prime example of ready wit.

Americans and Englishmen have never been able to comprehend each other's humor. Witness the number of smash London farce comedies that fall on their face every year on Broadway.

Being unable to understand Burgoyne's joke was so frustrating to the patriots that they decided to fortify Bunker's Hill, in Charlestown, from which Boston, a quarter of a mile away, would be a nice target.

By mistake they got onto Breed's Hill and threw up

a redoubt. So the Battle of Bunker Hill is really the Battle of Breed's Hill. I don't care. It's OK with me.

The patriot army headquarters were out in Cambridge in charge of a plodder from the French and Indian wars — General Artemas Ward. Cambridge, that quiet village across the Charles, was turned upside down. After Lexington a motley crew of ragtag and bobtail had converged on Cambridge from all over New England dragging their muskets if they had them, otherwise arriving with grandpa's cutlass, no food but an apple in one pocket and some corn bread in the other. They sprawled all over the town and their manners were rude.

Harvard College was dismissed and Stoughton, Hollis and other halls of the Crimson were used as barracks. The overflow slept under old sails or on the sidewalks in front of Leavitt and Pierce. President Langdon of Harvard was grieved by the profanity, shocking oaths, and imprecations of the new tenants. The college library was moved in wagons to Andover, Mass.

"Something," mused President Langdon, as the bust of Homer was loaded into a buckboard, "is afoot."

On the evening of June 16th, 1775, General Ward sent Colonel Prescott, with a detachment of 1000 men, down to Charlestown Neck and over to Bunker Hill. As stated they absentmindedly picked the wrong hill. Here they set to work and with pick and spade spent the whole night digging and issuing shocking oaths and imprecations. By sunrise the diggers had thrown up a fairly respectable redoubt and wanted food, water and relief. They got none of these because none had been ordered from Cambridge so they fit the Battle of Bunker Hill on empty stomachs and empty canteens and after working like hell all night.

At 4 A.M. the British ship *Lively*, twenty guns, spotted the activities up on the hill. Captain Thomas Bishop, who had recently been court martialled for neglect of duty, was in a peevish mood and without waiting for orders he opened fire in the total stillness of dawn.

Eighteenth century cannon were rather noisy. Boston woke up in a hurry.

Presently the other British ships in the harbor began to blast away. The noise was terrifying and many of the greenhorns on the hill wished at once that they were back in West Dover, Vermont, or Pow Wow River, New Hampshire, where things were quieter right then.

The ships bombarding our boys, who were still trying desperately to finish their earthworks, were the *Lively*, the *Falcon*, sixteen guns, the armed transport *Symmetry*, eighteen guns, and the *Glasgow*, twenty-four guns. Lucky for the rustics on the hill, the sixty-eight gun *Somerset* had been moved around to Hancock's Wharf only the day before.

Then in the rosy fingered dawn a shocking thing happened. A man working outside the redoubt was killed.

His name was Asa Pollard and he was decapitated by a cannon ball.

The lads gathered around. They had never seen a man without his head and they found it far from inspiring. A number of them decided they would prefer not to be in that kind of a fix and they went away from there, not stopping until they got to FITCHBURG.

Asa Pollard was buried. The remaining men went back to work and the bombardment continued. Now the British battery across the harbor on Copp's Hill opened up. The rooftops of Boston were covered with spectators.

The sun came up and the boys on the hill were now not only exhausted, hungry and thirsty, but hot. The officers urged Prescott to send to Cambridge for relief. His reply qualifies him for the Horatio Gates Prize for Military Lunacy.

"The men who have raised these works are the best able to defend them," he said.

The rest is history, but not the history I learned from Miss Sheridan and Miss Hagerty in Bryant School out on the banks of the Mississippi.

The British regulars in drill parade formation kept walking up that hill and the rebels kept mowing them down.

But behind the American lines was a perfect nuthouse. Soldiers without command wandered aimlessly as though they were at the Moose Club picnic. Officers with troops didn't know what to do with them.

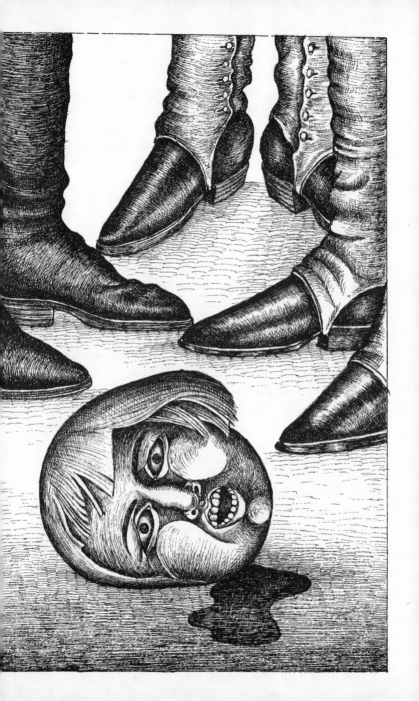

Some walked away from the fight, others ran. An artillery piece arrived but the cannonballs were the wrong size. Fat Colonel Samuel Gerrish, "unwieldy from excessive corpulence," lay on the ground wheezing. Entire companies deserted, led by their officers wearing track shoes.

Dr. Joseph Warren, the heart and soul of the rebellion and the noblest Roman on our side, arrived when the colonials were running out of powder. In the hand-to-hand fighting inside the redoubt he was killed. And that's why in the roster of American Presidents there is no President Warren.

(Ten months after the battle, Dr. Warren's body was dug up and identified by Paul Revere from two teeth he had installed in his friend.)

The bloodshed on the British side was sickening. The slaughter of officers was horrendous. Major Pitcairn lay dead. So did Major Spendlove, who had served forty years in the 43rd Regiment, to die for king and country where the elevated railroad now rumbles in the night. 89 officers in all were killed.

"That the officers suffered so much must be imputed to their being aimed at. . . . The dexterity which the Americans by long habit had acquired in hitting beasts, birds, and marks, was fatally applied to the destruction of our officers. From their fall much confusion was expected; they were, therefore, particularly singled out."

Out of gunpowder, our lads began a retreat, which became a rout and finally a calamity when a thousand stampeders squeezed into the only escape to the mainland, Charlestown Neck, barely 35 yards wide at its squeeze point.

Later the frogs began to croak and the moon came up.

Sir William Howe, Commander of the British, wounded, still lay on the battlefield, and spent the night there.

The army that held the field won the fight, according to the Queensberry Rules of the time. So the King had driven the rascals out of Charlestown and Wotan pressed the crown of victory onto his wig.

But there was no rejoicing across the bay in Boston which was filled with the English wounded and expiring.

Never in British military history had there been such a slaughter. Every American musket had dropped at least one man. Our English brothers had suffered 1100 casualties. That was one third of the crimson clad cohorts they had put in the field.

General Henry Clinton said it all.

"A dear bought victory," he said reviewing the carnage. "Another such would have ruined us."

Down in Virginia George Washington, that "profoundly British country gentleman," was riding to hounds on his farm, called "Mount Vernon."

Ask the Globe

Q. What kind of stone was used for the Bunker Hill Monument? — R.A., Charlestown.

A. Quincy granite, brought to Charlestown by barge and the first horse-drawn railroad cars used in the United States except for coal mines. The 221-foot obelisk was the first sizable monument in the United States but was erected in fits and starts. The Bunker Hill Association was formed in 1822 to buy a smaller battle monument and surrounding land from the Masonic Order.

The Marquis de Lafayette laid the cornerstone (later moved to the interior of the obelisk) and Daniel Webster made the oration at the cornerstone laying ceremonies in 1825. But progress under builder Solomon Willard lagged as funds ran dry. Finally, in 1840, a women's sewing circle initiated a seven-day fair at Quincy Market during the Whig Party convention. A total of $45,000 was raised, and two years later the capstone was lifted to the summit.

Boston *Globe*
May 23, 1973

Webster was a glorious windbag who could send patriotic clichés rumbling down Breed's Hill like hogsheads full of paving stones. His speech covers 16 pages of beautifully sliced *prosciutto*.

Marie Joseph Paul Yves Roch Gilbert Du Motier, Marquis de Lafayette, had survived the French revolution and years and years of French sauces, and George Washington's boy-wonder protégé was now a venerable sixty-eight years of age.

After the party at the monument he went over to Boston's Italian ghetto to the Old North Church. There was a bust there, which you can see today, of George Washington. The only way you can tell it's G. W. is because it says so. It looks a little like Sonny Tufts and a bit like Asst. Coach Gerald Ford and has a faint resemblance to Eddie Foy, Jr.

BUT, gazing on this marble, Lafayette said, and the sexton wrote it down on the back of a thanks offering envelope:

"Yes, that is the man I knew, and more like him than any other portrait."

Go and look at it. Was Lafayette full of Ward 8's or are all the other portraits of Washington wrong?

The admission to the Bunker Hill monument is 10¢. For this sum you can hasten a reluctant heart attack by climbing 295 claustrophobic steps.

But the view from the top is inspiring, as it encompasses miles and miles of frame tenements, red brick parochial schools, and the Jordan Marsh warehouse.

The Ward 8, a cocktail whose vogue has long been on the wane, was invented in and named for Boston's 8th Ward.

☞ SIX ☜

PATRICK HENRY as a youth was very indolent and dull. But in March 1775 he snapped out of it and hollered "Give Me Liberty Or Give Me Death!" Everybody was surprised at him.

On May 10th Ethan Allen and Benedict Arnold with 83 Green Mountain Boys captured British forts at Ticonderoga and Crown Point. Strange doings, since we were not at war with England. About 150 cannon were grabbed in this sneaky way, and later on were dragged all the way to Boston, via Athol and Fitchburg, where they were helpful in persuading Lord Howe to move out.

I went up to Ticonderoga last month to research the fort. I am a very meticulous historian as you may have gathered by now. I discovered that (a) the fort is a replica and (b) the admission fee is $2.00. I have still not seen Fort Ticonderoga, as I am also a meticulous tightwad.

On the same day Ticonderoga was captured, the SECOND CONTINENTAL CONGRESS convened in Philadelphia.

First they had a contest to see who could write his own name the biggest. John Hancock won and was elected President of the Congress.

Next they framed a conciliatory letter to King George telling him they were sorry they had made him sore and hoped things could be patched up. George was so vexed by then that he refused even to read this document: it was his last chance to hold the colonies and eventually get taxes from the Campbell's Soup Co. conglomerate.

They then voted to raise an army of 20,000 men. And for starters, they officially named that incongruous mass of undisciplined dubs then milling about in Cambridge the CONTINENTAL ARMY.

Two days before the battle of Bunker Hill, John Adams got up and proposed GEORGE WASHINGTON for Commander-in-Chief. Adams did it for purely political reasons — to butter up the southern colonies and keep them interested in throwing brickbats at Parliament in concert with the other colonies.

About ten minutes after nominating Washington, John Adams began to loathe and detest him which he continued to do all his life. He picked at him all during the war, he picked at him as President, and he picked at him after he was dead and he picked at Martha and all the Washington family.

"Taxation without representation" was mentioned a few times and then everybody went to lunch. They no doubt had a point. However, based on the representation we've been seeing on the tube from Washington the last year or so I wouldn't invite any representation to a dog fight. And if I did, they'd probably figure out some way to throw the fight.

By the time George Washington got to Cambridge the place looked like a Rock Festival that had been going on for 2½ months. The "army" had taken everything except baths, including a number of trollops, jades, and trulls.

After first contact with his legions Washington wrote home that they were "dirty and nasty people." With the aid of General Horatio Gates (late of His Majesty's imperial forces) he began to whip them into shape. He worked on this for the next eight years with minimum results.

He also began to tighten the siege of Boston and soon had Lord Howe in the cage.

The American command, Washington present and voting, then was seized with the dizzy notion that our Canadian brothers, Loyalists all, could be persuaded to join our crusade against England and boiled cabbage if we would just go up there and shoot at them with guns.

The idea that you can change people's minds with artillery has always been basic in the American Dream.

General Richard Montgomery with a body of New England and New York troops started for Montreal and had good luck. It wasn't easy, nothing was easy in 1775 except breathing, but he took St. Jean, Chambly (named by Edward Lear), and eventually Montreal.

In a skirmish preceding the fall of Montreal, Ethan Allen made the wrong move, got himself captured, and was sent to England in chains to cool off. He was released in 1778 but never saw action again.

So far so good. (Except for Allen.)

But Washington's pet project, on the other side of the reservation, was running into plenty trouble. He had thought it would be great if about a thousand intrepid Americans would make their way up through the wilderness of northern Maine and down the Chaudière River, pop out on the St. Lawrence and yell "Boo" at the fortress of Quebec. He and his board of strategy were completely convinced that the "element of surprise" would be so devastating that the gates of the citadel would swing open and the Americans all be invited in to dinner at the Château Frontenac, complete with sodden *chou de Bruxelles*.

Now as anyone knows, it is impossible even now to go through northern Maine to Quebec. In summer the roads are blocked with Airstream trailers, and in winter with Volkswagens from New Jersey with skis on top. In those days there was nothing at all except rocks, rapids, mountains, bogs, and the perpetual gloom of the fearsome forest and the cruelties of nature.

Washington picked the only man for the job who could have got through: Benedict Arnold. I might as well admit that I am all for Benedict Arnold, and I'm only sorry that he turned out to be a cad. Benedict happened to have some elements in his character typical of an Ann Page yuletide fruit cake; but he provided some much needed Kolor to an often poky and numbing script. And when it came to Brave, he was actually a lunatic in the Fearless department.

He also married the All-Colony Beauty Queen, a heavenly tomato from Philly called Margaret Shippen. Margaret was a Tory, slightly hysterical, and they made a deliciously daffy duet.

Benedict was 120 proof. He was a pistol.

Well buddy, you just blew your royalties from the "additional reading" school list. And you can expect the pickets from the D.A.R. most any time. I don't care. But don't try to tie tin cans to my dog's tail. He is a bullterrier and will eat you alive.

Arnold and his men went up the Kennebec River as far as it would go. They had the wrong kind of bateaux which started falling apart after about ten days of banging on rocks and portaging. Soldiers are not boatmen and some drowned, others died of pneumonia. A few sat on wet logs under the dripping spruce trees and died of discouragement.

They entered the Dead River and it began to snow. They waded through icy swamps up to their armpits. The food started giving out. It was very cold.

Arnold drove them on to the Height of Land.

The troops in the rear, under the dastardly Colonel Enos, turned tail and deserted, 500 strong, returning to home and Mother with all their provisions. Enos was court martialled. But only slightly.

Arnold got over the mountains to the headwaters of the Chaudière. This river is a bitch. More men drowned. They ate all their dogs. They fricasseed their moosehide moccasins.

Moral grandeur is what the text books call this kind of behavior. It is actually a form of insanity. But Arnold and Washington were pikers. The Pentagon spends 13 billion $ $ $ a day. And we all Love It and we all Want More.

On November 9th what was left of the scarecrow army arrived on the St. Lawrence.

"Les voilà! Ils sont arrivés," said the Quebecois across the river. They had been expecting the Americans for some time.

So much for Washington's "element of surprise."

Nothing daunted, this crazy s.o.b. Arnold got 500 men across that wide unpleasant river at night and crawled up to the Plains of Abraham. With only 400 muskets and no artillery he drew up in front of the enormous fortress the next day and demanded total surrender of the city, the garrison, and all the *habitant* pea soup within the walls.

This offer was rejected and Arnold retreated to Pointe aux Trembles where he and the boys spent a trembly three weeks until Montgomery arrived from Montreal with support and some woolens.

On New Year's Eve of 1775 the American forces attacked the mighty bastion in the middle of a raging blizzard. Once again the element of surprise failed to pan out. Noble Montgomery was killed. Benedict Arnold was badly wounded. Captain Daniel Morgan, the old campaigner, was captured with all his men.

Arnold's remainders spent the rest of a typical un-friendly Canadian winter at Sillery. They attacked again in April. No dice. The British now took the offensive.

By mid-June the Americans had been driven com-pletely out of Canada, retreating so fast that they left all their stores and sick behind them.

Thus ended one of the most grotesque campaigns in military records. A story of bravery pushed close to the boundaries of lunacy — hardship and death — all rewarded with abysmal failure.

And the ironic part is — the night they arrived in front of the massive walls of the fortress of Quebec, the St. Jean gate was wide open. The could have walked right in.

But they decided to wait until morning.

And years later, in the reigns of John Quincy Adams, and even Andrew Jackson, curly haired tots were wont to climb on the laps of grizzled veterans of that campaign and beg:

"Pleath Grampa tell uth thum more about theventeen theventy thix when you wath with Benedick Armwold and eating the puppy dogth and the thnowthtorm at Keebeck thity and all that thtuff."

Headlines of 1776

E. Gibbon: *Decline and Fall of the Roman Empire*.
Vienna *Burgtheater* founded.
Torture abolished in Austria.
Adam Smith: *Wealth of Nations*.
Viceroyalty of River Plate established.
John Constable born.
Lady Hester Stanhope born.
David Hume dies.
Julie de Lespinasse dies.
Lord Moncreiff born.
Abolition of Forced Road Labor in France.
Russia cedes claims to Holstein.
Free trade in corn abolished in France.
Potemkin, favorite of Catherine II, organizes Russian
    Black Sea fleet.
James Cook's third voyage of discovery in the Pacific.
J. H. Fragonard paints "The Washerwoman."

☞ SEVEN ☜

ALL THIS TIME George Washington had the British boxed in, bottled up, and damn mad in Boston. The unhappy city contained a mince pie stuffing consisting of Tories, Patriots, British soldiers, mountebanks and black marketeers. Food was scarce, the sacred town bull was slaughtered. The North Meeting House was burned for fuel.

Paul Revere remained at his old stand, however, hammering out silver porringers and spoons for the Parke Bernet and Sotheby auctions. Revere must have turned out several million spoons in his time as every family on the eastern seaboard has at least one. And there are more Paul Revere spoons in the antique stores than splinters of the True Cross in Spain.

Sir William Howe was now top limejuicer in Boston. He had a roaming eye which soon after his arrival had landed full force on toothsome Elizabeth Lloyd Loring. Skyrockets and pinwheels were soon going off and the earth moved for William and Elizabeth. A bard later commemorated this tender romance in lyric form. A fragment will suffice.

> *"Sir William, he, snug as a flea,*
> *Lay all this time a-snoring;*
> *Nor dreamed of harm, as he lay warm*
> *In bed with Mrs. Loring . . ."*

Back in England Parliament finally awakened from rosy dreams of imperial puissance and realized it had a nasty scrap on its hands. To cope with Whiggish mischief abroad it voted a land and naval force of 55,000 men and more than a million dollars to support them. It also, which flabbergasts our democratic minds to this day, *hired* 17,000 soldiers from the Landgrave of Hesse-Cassel and other small-time kraut despots. This act "filled the cup of government inequity to the brim."

Washington was living in Craigie House in Cambridge, later the home of Longfellow and open today for your inspection, admission 50¢, No Smoking, Please Wipe Your Feet. He was lonesome for Martha and she came from Mount Vernon to cold clammy Massachusetts. She brought with her some prize goods from a captured merchant vessel: oranges, limes, lemons, sweetmeats and pickles. Martha could not get used to the distant cannonading but she stayed through the winter of 1775–76. She then went home but rejoined the army for the dreadful winter of 1776–77 at Morristown.

The siege of Boston dragged on.

And then the drummer hit some rim shots, there was a puff of smoke, and Henry Knox bowed in to History.

As a future hero Henry had certain natural advantages. For one thing he became in time a "youth." But Henry Knox was not just a plain "youth" he was a "youth" with a "widowed mother" whose support fell on Henry, thereby making him into an instant "plucky youth."

Henry hired out pluckily to work "long hours," with "no complaint," in a "dusty book store." (A book store with no dust opened in Howard St. in Boston in 1764 but soon closed due to cleanliness.)

Henry also had sickening Rollo-ish tendencies, for in addition to unpacking books and putting them in stock & c. he developed the habit of *reading* them. I believe he even read them "voraciously."

His specialty became military history especially the science of artillery which is cannons on wheels, cannon balls, explosions and the like.

Knox eventually opened his own dusty book store in Cornhill, called "The London Book Store." It became highly fashionable and a daily meeting place for the bon ton of Beantown, as well as for the Officers of King George's Army of Occupation, than whom nothing on earth could be more gaudy or have more outlandish accents.

Mamas towed their blushing, bouncing daughters in to giggle at the pretty bindings and flutter fans at the officers of the Royal Irish or the Lancashires.

Henry Knox, genial prop., charmed everyone. And between bowing and twinkling out front, was often in the back room with some British officer arguing points of artillery. Such as, the battle of Oudenaarde, 1708. Such as, the Battle of Lützen, 1632.

Henry was fat. He weighed 280 pounds but he was handsome and carried his poundage with aplomb. Adorable, plump Miss Lucy Flucker became an ardent bibliophile after meeting the pleasing proprietor and they were soon in love. This was not so simple because Henry was a Patriot and Lucy's father was a stuffy, perfectly dreadful Tory and the royal secretary to the Massachusetts colony. One imagines the scene that followed:

"Mr. Flucker, sir, I have come to ask your daughter Lucy's hand in marriage."

"Egad! Such insolence, sir! How dare you suggest a union with the house of Flucker?"

"But Mr. Flucker . . ."

True love had its way and while furious Flucker fumed, Henry and Lucy were married, in June 1774. A year later, after Lexington and Concord, Henry closed the doors of his bookstore, assisted Lucy into a carriage, and they drove through the British lines at Roxbury and did not return.

Henry never saw his stock of books again.

Lucy never saw her parents again.

The bookstore was ransacked and the books stolen. The Fluckers vamoosed to Nova Scotia with General Howe's flotilla, and subsequently to England.

Knox and Lucy repaired to Cambridge and requested an audience with General Washington.

Now Washington, on assuming his new role of Commander-in-Chief of the Continental Army, had *not* been overly cordial to most of the New Englanders who had presented themselves to him requesting instant military rank, titles and pay. Washington was not just a southern aristocrat he was a soldier. He didn't see why the fire chief of Haverhill, Mass., should subito become a Lieutenant Colonel in the army.

It was different with Knox.

Henry was busting out all over with personality. And, from books at least, he knew more about artillery than anybody around.

There was also Lucy.

George Washington liked girls. When only a schoolboy he had been caught "romping with one of the largest girls." He had ever since enjoyed having girls around, especially pretty ones. He liked Lucy a whole lot.

On one occasion he danced with her for three hours

non-stop. Martha by this time was of a matronly size and perfectly happy to sit on the side lines watching George have a good time. Lucy herself was a stylish stout, in the prime of young womanhood, and she loved to dance.

Martha's dancing slippers, pale blue silk, are in the museum at Morristown. They're cute.

Look at George Washington on the dollar bill and he doesn't look much like a truckin' fool, but he was.

General Nathanael Greene married pretty Kitty Littlefield of Block Island. Kitty was a merry madcap who kept everybody in stitches. The Commander-in-Chief of the entire Colonial Army, later First President of the United States, once led Kitty onto the birch flooring and whirled her around for *four hours* without missing a beat.

Washington danced throughout the Revolution. Henry Knox describes a typical modest soiree: ". . . we had above seventy ladies, all of the first ton in the State, and between three and four hundred gentlemen. We danced all night . . ."

George was still picking them up and putting them down in 1796 at the age of 64. But he sent his regrets to the Alexandria Assembly in 1799, saying, "Mrs. Washington and I have been honored . . . But, alas! our dancing days are no more."

Where were we?
Cambridge. Washington's headquarters. 1775.

Truckin George

Washington made Knox a colonel and chief of the Continental artillery. All grand — except there was practically no artillery to command.

For a bookseller and a bookworm Knox was a ball of fire and suggested to Washington that he would be glad to go over to Ticonderoga and bring back the British artillery captured by Ethan Allen and Benedict Arnold. George thought that was OK if it could be done. But of course it couldn't.

Colonel Knox went to Ticonderoga three hundred miles from Boston, way over on Lake George, which today has more motels and gift shoppes than Lake Tahoe but which at that time was pretty barren. The Karmelkorn Korner, for example, didn't open until 1791.

Knox picked out 59 pieces. (The rest had had it and were wore out.) They weighed 120,000 pounds. With a caravan of 42 sledges hauled by 80 yoke of oxen the rotund bookseller started for Boston. It was late December and they had to cross the Berkshires and the entire state of Massachusetts.

"Another dern fool notion" was the native opinion of this project, and everybody went back into the house for another piece of dried apple pie.

Early in February Knox appeared in Cambridge with the guns.

"General, I have brought you a noble train of artillery," he said.

"Bodacious work, sir!" replied Washington.

"Oh Henry!" cried Lucy. "Oh Henry!"

"Say, you know what?" Washington remarked thoughtfully. "That would make a great name for a candy bar!"

Washington promptly lined up the cannon on Dorchester Heights. From here they could shoot down upon the British regulars in Boston in a very impertinent way.

General Howe pondered briefly on the advisability of attacking Dorchester Heights. Remembering the sanguinary showdown at Bunker Hill he decided to evacuate. Mrs. Loring agreed. She and Lord Howe went back to bed but only for a short time.

The abandonment of Boston and departure by boat was an exercise in organized confusion.

Think what a family of four has to go through just to pack the car and go up to good old Mud Lake for the weekend.

Here we had to load 11,000 people on 100 ships; and every person wanted to bring his tennis racquet, his record player, his cat, his water skis, his saxophone, his sewing machine, his collapsible camp stove, etc. 1100 Loyalists had made the awesome decision to cut the home ties, part with New England and leave with the army.

The wealthier ones naturally wished to salvage as many of the family treasures as they could. They even took furniture aboard the waiting warships.

Howe came aboard to find the decks littered with these chattels and consigned them to the deep. Boston harbor was soon suffering dreadful pollution from a large coagulum of Queen Anne escritoires, Chippendale side chairs, Hepplewhite commodes, Wagstaffe case clocks, chinoiserie knee hole desks, and ormolu ormolus, all bobbing around in the brine and coming unglued.

Very sad.

Remember, Tories, or Loyalists, were not Britons living in Boston. They were Americans, some of them unto the fifth generation. Their forefathers had suffered, more than it seems necessary for people to have done, during the hellish morbid years of 17th Century New England. They had endured the plague of the Mathers, Cotton and Increase, a visitation more dread than the Black Death. They had been through this and worse: redskins, witches, 4 hour sermons, hasty pudding.

They had never been to Selfridge's white sales or to the pantomime at the Palladium. They had never been in England. They were Americans but they were British subjects loyal to King, the white cliffs of Dover, steak and kidney pie, and gooseberry fool.

For this loyalty the ones who left Boston paid an awful penalty. They lost everything and gained nothing. Dumped in Nova Scotia, they found themselves set back 150 years, only at an even more desolate site than Plymouth.

Those who could get to England found themselves strangers, ignored and unemployable.

Washington and the army stood on the heights of Dorchester and watched as over 100 of His Majesty's ships made sail and headed down Nantasket Roads.

It was nine months since that sunny June day when the waving grasses of Bunker Hill had run with rivulets of red.

The British had left Boston. They would never return.

Except as tourists to see the glass flowers in the Museum at Harvard.

George Washington's Health

In George Washington's family there was a history of tuberculosis and he himself probably had it. He was a chronic sufferer from colds, ear, nose and throat troubles, night sweats, chronic cough, pressure on chest, shortness of breath, indigestion, stomach and liver trouble, and carbuncles. He had agonizing tooth troubles and was probably unable to chew any hard foods properly. Some of his case history includes: Malaria, 1749; Small pox, 1751; tubercular pleurisy, 1751–52; influenza, 1755; malaria, 1754; dysentery, 1757; malaria, 1761; dysentery, 1767. Doctors presume he had chronic infected tonsils.

American Heritage

☞ **EIGHT** ☜

WHEN HE EVACUATED Boston why did General Howe take his fleet to Nova Scotia instead of to New York?

Because Howe was the type who was constantly arriving at the trolley stop in the midnight rain to see the Owl Car disappearing out of sight.

So he went north, having read the Boston and Maine R.R. brochures about the invigorating air and sport fishing of the Maritime Provinces.

Washington bade farewell to Craigie House and to steamed codfish cheeks at the Parker House. He went south via the Boston Post Road and occupied New York. Although this trip only took Washington personally three days, if you read the guidebooks you will find that he slept in over 125 different houses.

Things had not been quiet in the South.

In addition to the usual Saturday night pully-haulys

over politics, horses and women at the corner saloon, there had been a couple of weirdo battles.

The back country inland from Wilmington, North Carolina, is the usual barren sandy scrub and pitch pine they call "land" in the Southeast. The most prominent feature today is rusty tin roofs and road signs of the type that say BURGAW 11 M.

They had a battle here. I went over to look at the grounds. The gov't has fixed it up some and put a cannon there but somebody stole it.

March 1776:

In North Carolina there were a lot of Scottish clans who, since they belonged to the human race, wanted to fight about something. It seems that the various varieties of Celts are just as barmy as Anglo Saxons in matters of politics. Although they had been kicked bodily out of Scotland after the battle of Culloden and transported thousands of miles from the Highland distilleries by George II, they now decided to support George III, who loathed haggis and said rude things about Flora Macdonald and Bobbie Burns.

The reason for this is probably that they were mad at the other colonials because of taking a constant ribbing about their kilts and all the time being asked what kind of underpants they had on.

A bunch of them were headed for the coast to join up with the King's troops. So they could wield their oversize double-bitted claymores in behalf of the detested house of Hanover if you can believe such an example of human perversity.

With bagpipes squeaking, kilts flying, bare knees twinkling in the breeze, these braw lads ran head on into a team of colonials under Caswell and Lillington at Moores Creek Bridge. "Caswell and Lillington" sounds like a high class set of undertakers. It turned out they were.

Moores Creek was and is a dark, sluggish stream about five feet deep. It lacked distinction. There was a little bridge there, which turned out to be historic. Anybody looking at it before the battle would not have given two cents for it. You never know.

The patriots, 1000 highly assorted ring-tailed militia, threw up a long serpentine embankment on the west side. This embankment is still there and is so low that a dachshund standing behind it could get his ears shot off.

The militia then stripped the floor planks off the bridge and greased the girders.

At daybreak the Scots wha hae cried aloud "King George and Broad Swords!" and rushed the bridge.

It would have been funny if it hadn't been so pathetic and so gory.

While the Scots on the slippery bridge timbers (Jimmy Finlayson, Snub Pollard, Stan Laurel, etc.) skidded, pirouetted, and did expert Mack Sennett pratfalls, the militia poured on these sorry bit players a "withering" fire of musket and artillery.

Three minutes it took. Nearly all the Celts were wiped out. Moores Creek, as creeks have been wont to do since Man first belted his neighbor over the head, turned crimson. The Highlanders who were not dead on the bridge, in the water, or on the bank, went away from there, dragging their claymores behind them but omitting the bagpiping.

Within two weeks all of these loyalists and their gear had been captured together with a surprise bonus of $75,000 in gold.

What did it all prove?

1. The Tory clans were all washed up.

2. Other Loyalists in North and South Carolina decided they better not start anything funny.

3. Revolutionary excitement got a big shot in the arm all the way to Meddybemps, Maine.

4. Beginning in the year 1926 the battlefield has been giving steady employment to a sizeable number of employees of the National Park Service.

The other battle in the South, in June 1776, was down the coast at Charleston. This was the only great American port south of Philadelphia.

Two British fleets, one under General Clinton, the other under Lord Cornwallis Cornwallis, had been having a jolly cruise up and down the coast, singing the old songs, playing pranks on the cook, and trying to find something to shoot at.

On June 28 they picked Sullivans Island at Charleston, S. C., now Fort Moultrie.

The fleet immediately went into a comedy act.

Ships collided, ships ran aground, ships got into the wrong channel, ships blocked each other's range. Infantry ordered to attack across a shallow gut found the water seven feet deep. Admiral Peter Parker actually had his pants blown off.

The gunners in the fort were raising hell with the sluggish, floundering flotilla. Rigging went down, masts went overboard.

An officer described H.M.S. *Bristol:*

"No slaughterhouse could present so bad a sight with blood and entrails lying about, as our ship."

The fort itself was an insult. All the King's terrible fire power could not dent it.

It was made of the only materials at hand: double walls of palmetto logs, with sand in between. Old Albion's most fearsome rotund projectiles simply squashed into the mushy palmetto and buried themselves in the sand with dull thuds.

"Curses!" groaned the gunnery officers. "Foiled again by the devilish colonial ingenuity."

The British ships retired in disorderly dismay. It was the greatest American defensive victory in the whole war. British losses: 225. American losses: 2.

Charleston was saved. The ladies' Garden Club went back to planning the next Magnolia Festival.

It was a busy month — June 1776. On the 7th Richard Henry Lee of Virginia arose in the Continental Congress and read the fatal Resolution:

"That these united colonies are, and, of right, ought to be free and independent states; that they are absolved from all allegiance to the British crown . . ."

A vote was taken in Heaven, and God decided not to demolish the Congress and Philadelphia with a lightning bolt. Many had expected it, and were huddled in crude "Lord's wrath shelters" near Walnut Street.

The rest of the month was spent in Thomas Jefferson's writing the DECLARATION OF INDEPENDENCE. And in Ben Franklin and John Adams blue pencilling it, with some kibitzing from Robert Livingston of New York and Roger Sherman of Connecticut. (Roger Sherman was named for the Roger Sherman Soda Spa, across the street from the Taft Hotel in New Haven.)

In the original version Jefferson blamed the King for slavery, "this assemblage of horrors." The others said this was going too far, George had nothing to do with it. Strange chap, Jefferson. He owned 83 slaves at the time.

Then there is his noble phrase, "All men are created equal." Naturally Jefferson was not referring to Ethiopians, Indians, Tartars, Israelites, Finns, Zulus, Micks, Armenians, Sicilians, or Tierra del Fuegians. They were not men, they were not even people in his view.

The *Declaration of Independence* was a big success and people immediately began to do very silly things.

In Boston the "King's arms were taken down from the State House and every vestige of him from every place." Instead of having an auction and selling these valuable trophies to the antique dealers, they had a bonfire and burnt them up.

There was also a good deal of drinking.

And that's why the United States had 356 highway fatalities last Fourth of July.

Eggs à la Washington

Make four omelets of 4 eggs each, one with apples, one with asparagus or sorrel (according to the season), a third with *fines herbes,* and the fourth *au naturel;* you serve them on the same dish, one lapping over the other. It makes a fine as well as a good dish.

This omelet, or rather these omelets, were a favorite dish with the Father of his Country; they were very often served on his table when he had a grand dinner. It is also served with the four following omelets: *au naturel,* with salt pork, *fines herbes,* and with cheese.

PIERRE BLOT
Hand-Book of Practical Cookery
1868

☞ NINE ☜

ONE OF THE MOST frequent pictorial effects of the Revolution was the view of the militia running for home before, during, and after battles. There were usually few left to run away after battles because they had already made themselves scarce before or during.

"My mother needs me to split kindlins," one would say as he went over the hill.

"My folks is all out of apple butter," was another hot one, "and I'm the oney one knows how to make it."

"My shoestring is broke. I'll be right back as soon as I get a new one."

Washington was sore about this all the time and blew up frequently as he had a very short fuse.

After getting bounced out of New York and being kicked clear across New Jersey to the far side of the Delaware River, Washington had lost so many men captured and deserted that he was in the dumps.

He wrote his favorite brother, John Augustine (whom he addressed as "Dear Jack"):

"I think the game is pretty nearly up."

The New York campaign was a turkey on Washington's part.

What was he thinking of? Was he thinking at all? What about? The fall plowing at Mount Vernon?

If Howe had not as usual dropped the ball it would have been the end of the war and today the Ladies' Page editors throughout our land would fall into a dead faint on hearing the words "Princess Anne."

Washington and his entourage went down from New England to New York and fanned out all over the place. Washington was living at the corner of Charlton and Varick Sts. General John Sullivan was in digs on Brooklyn Heights. Earnest, plodding Israel Putnam was in a cheap but clean boarding house near the Bowery. Nathanael Greene zigzagged around from Coney Island to East Rockaway and occasionally dropped in to see the boys on Fire Island. Henry Knox was at Number 1, Broadway.

Washington put the lads to work fortifying Brooklyn Heights and a lot of other places.

Erecting fortifications served two important functions aside from the fact that they might be useful. (One half the time they were useless, as the enemy went someplace else.)

1. It gave the men something to do besides play mumblety-peg and tell dirty stories.

2. It gave the officers the feeling that they were playing at war according to grand principles. Surveying a squad of men digging a trench and crying, "Well done, lads!" gave them a personal warlike glow.

Lucy Flucker Knox had come down to visit Henry at Number 1 Broadway and they were spooning in the front parlor.

"Oh Henry, look at all those ships," Lucy exclaimed.

Three British fleets had arrived, and they deposited 34,000 warriors on Staten Island.

This was the largest expeditionary force ever landed on the shores of North or South America. The amiable Montross says there were 52 warships and 427 transports, including a number of "ships of the line." These enormous vehicles carried as many as 136 guns. Nelson's *Victory* displayed 108. Naval battles in those peculiar times were fought in opposing columnar formations of heavy warships. This was called "line ahead." Hence "line of battle" ships or "ships of the line."

The 34,000 redcoats around their camp fires near the Staten Island ferry slip were greater in number than England, two generations later, would be able to send across the Channel to Waterloo.

Lucy Knox took the night train for Boston.

Washington had about 20,000 men scattered around in Brooklyn and Manhattan.

On 27 August 1776, General Howe attacked Long Island. Instead of staying in the carefully prepared fortifications on Brooklyn Heights, Washington decided to fight it out on the plain. No one will ever know why. The British specialty was open-field fighting, the Americans were in blissful ignorance on the subject.

The American troops were placed all wrong and took a terrible pasting. As usual, the militia panicked and ran away, almost knocking down General Washington in their flight.

The Americans lost 1300 men in killed, wounded, and captured.

They would have lost the whole army and the war would have been over, but now it was Howe's turn to play the juggins. He withdrew and got up a game of euchre with Clinton and Cornwallis.

The next day the fight was called on account of rain.

On the night of August 28th, Washington executed a "strategic retirement" and succeeded in ferrying 9000 men, artillery, horses, cattle, cuirasses, halberds, bucklers and other warlike impedimenta across the river to Manhattan, the present day Fun City of the World.

Washington and his forces were in a precarious and very drafty position. Army morale was at low tide. Whoring, armed robbery, bestial conduct and rampageous behavior were on the loose, giving that ineffable tone to the city which it has proudly clung to through the years.

On September 15, after a heavy naval bombardment, British troops landed at Kips Bay, near 34th Street.

Washington rushed to the scene. The militia had again been seized with anxiety as to what was going on at home and were proceeding rapidly in that direction. And once again they collided with the Commander-in-Chief. Washington let loose one of his only public temper tantrums of the war, cursed them for "dastardly cowards" and whacked a few with the flat of his sword. They kept on hustling west.

Washington had had enough Fun and decided to get out. The British grabbed the Boston Post Road so he had to go up Broadway which was then called the Bloomingdale Road. Putnam and his troops made their way through farms and footpaths north and joined Washington at 59th Street near the present site of the New York Athletic Club.

While this was going on Mrs. Robert Murray invited General Howe and his officers to tea. So as the enemy hightailed it up the island, the top British brass engaged in small talk and nibbled on pound cake, jam tarts and lady fingers. Mrs. Murray also brought out some fine Madeira.

Washington took a stand on Harlem Heights at 125th Street. He held off the British in a small engagement, and retreated to White Plains. Five rounds. No decision. Washington crossed the Hudson and continued to retire strategically, at full gallop, clear down through Hackensack, Newark, New Brunswick, and Trenton with the British hot on his heels.

On December 8, 1776, Washington was shoved with what was left of his army to the Pennsylvania side of the Delaware River. Of the 20,000 men he had had in August he had only 5,000 left.

Everything seemed to have gone blooey. We had been kicked out of New York — Fort Washington and Fort Lee had been captured with lots of men and kill material — for months Washington had made nothing but one blooper after another — and to top it all off General Charles Lee, the only real professional in American ranks, had been captured under ridiculous circumstances.

Howe figured he had the war about wrapped up and decided to spend the winter in New York going to cocktail parties and Opening Nights on the booze and bang circuit, and taking Mrs. Loring to the six day bike races. He would finish Washington off in the spring.

Down in dreary New Jersey he left troops of occupation who made life miserable for the inhabitants, looting everything in sight, tumbling the girls, burning houses, and giving the folks their first taste of churlish military manners both German and English.

Occupation of New Jersey by rapacious British troops and their Hessian hirelings maddened everyone and converted not a few rabid Tories into flaming indignant Patriots.

". . . so here Gen¹ How had fast hold of us by the beard of conquest with one hand to kiss us with his good orders while, with his Cruel bad orders he gave us a Mortal Blow and shed out our bowels to ye ground by their Insults Roberys & Plunderings."

Washington was much worse off than Lord Howe suspected. Colonial enlistments would be up on January 1st and the army would practically disappear. By ten minutes past midnight on that date George Washington's command would number less than 1400 men. His entire army wouldn't fill the Majestic theater in Dubuque.

Washington stood on the bank of the ice-choked Delaware pondering. It was snowing, sleeting, windy, miserable, and the men had no tents, no blankets, no food, and somebody had even lost the deck of cards.

Across the river in Trenton the sneering, contemptuous Hessians were essen und fressen und trinken their ponderous way through a heavily Germanic and bibulous Christmas.

Suddenly a small balloon appeared over George Washington's head containing a lighted lanthorn.

The King
We Love to Hate
George the Third
of England
The Ogre

Liked to gossip with country folk.

Set a model of royal domesticity which has lasted to this day.

Founded the Indian empire.

Defended Gibraltar against continuous assault.

Fought Napoleon for 20 years and mashed him at Waterloo.

Founded the British Museum.

Preferred Benjamin West to Joshua Reynolds.

Founded the Royal Academy.

IN HIS REIGN

Britain's population doubled.

Britain's wealth zoomed.

Steam engine, spinning jenny and power loom in-
    vented.
The railroad arrived on the scene.
Britain became the greatest manufacturing country in
    the world.
His reign second longest in British history.

". . . few kings have shown greater courage both moral
    and physical. . . ." *Encyclopaedia Britannica.*

☞ TEN ☜

CELEBRATING CHRISTMAS had become such a rowdy affair in England that it was outlawed by Act of Parliament in 1644.

In the grim New England colonies the Puritans followed suit with their customary monomania. December 25th was just another day of unsmiling drudgery. There was a 5 shilling fine for anyone nibbling plum pudding on the sly or humming "Good King Wenceslaus" out behind the barn. By the blue laws of the Massachusetts Bay Colony *mince pies* were actually banned as smacking of Popery and Yuletide delinquency. Slimy, nasty, nauseous Cotton Mather added "wanton Bacchanallian Christmasses" to his ever-lengthening Sin and Damnation List. Thus did our amiable forefathers ruin the retail business in tin soldiers and doll houses in their loony fanaticism to "beat down every sprout of Episcopacie."

Fools! Flatheads! I would like to shove Bloomingdale's December sales records down their canting craws. Or Marshall Field's.

By 1700 the Church of England in the Colonies had reinstated the Christmas service and even decorated the church with greens. The Puritans ranted, raved, and behaved as usual like complete stiffs.

But still, even in very English Virginia, Christmas as the spectacle we know it did not exist. Nobody exchanged gifts of bath salts and electric carving knives. There were no Christmas trees. Santa Claus was still confining his enterprise to North European chimneys. Dickensian bathos, on this Christmas Day in 1776, was exactly 67 years in the future.

It was different with the hated Hessian hirelings across the river and G. Washington knew it. They not only "kept Christmas" but it was perfectly plain that being Huns they would do everything to excess and could now be counted upon to indulge in total *Schlemmerei* and *Trunkensucht*. In other words eat like pigs and get as drunk as Indians.*

Say, what was a "Hessian" anyway?

"Hessians" was a term used loosely to describe the German mercenaries who fought on the British side in the Revolutionary War. Most of them came from the German principalities of Hesse-Cassel, Hesse-Hanau, Brunswick, Waldeck, Anspach-Bayreuth and Anhalt-Zerbst.

---

* Put that gun down, Marlon, or I'll ventilate you so you look like a Swiss cheese.

The whole thing was slightly disgusting and many of the British, both people and parliamentarians, considered it a nasty business.

Who was more despicable — a King who would hire slave soldiers of another country to kill people of his own pedigree across the seas, or a ruler in the business of selling his own people's blood to line his personal pockets with gold? The Landgrave of Hesse-Cassel had 106 children to support and in order to keep them in pony carts and sugar plums he stripped his country of one fourth of its able bodied men and sold them for the sum of £3,000,000.

According to Article IX of the agreement with his Britannic majesty, ". . . Three wounded men shall be reckoned as one killed. A man killed shall be paid for at the rate of the levy money . . ."

Thus the German rulers did not rejoice in British victories from the use of German troops, quite the contrary. The more dead Hessians, the bigger the payoff. Lovely people, as we all found out in 1939.

In the disastrous New York campaign, Fort Washington was assaulted and captured by Hessian troops under General Knyphausen.

"This sort of glory, won by German mercenaries against free-born English subjects has no charms for me," said Edmund Burke in Parliament.

In all, King George rented 30,000 German souls, paying out £4,700,000. Of this number 12,000 never returned across the sea. 7000 were killed or turned up missing. 5000 deserted and went to Milwaukee.

The Hessian troops sent over in 1776 were probably the finest military regiments in the world, all drilled on the Prussian system and under command of superb officers like Eric von Stroheim. Britain put her finest regiments in the field here, the 17th Light Dragoons, the 71st Highlanders, the 33rd Foot, the Royal Welsh Fusiliers, the Coldstream Guards, but none of them had anything on the Hessian Jäger Corps in a fight.

Elisha Bostwick of the Seventh Connecticut Regiment describes "the personal appearance of a Hessian":

"They are of moderate stature, rather broad shoulders, light complexion with a blueish tinge, hair cued as tight to the head as possible, sticking straight back like the handle of an iron skillet."

At Trenton our ragabash army learned that it could dance like a butterfly, sting like a bee, and that even the majestic Hessians could be slugged to their knees.

So Washington crossed the Delaware.

Yale students, the sharpest in the land, were recently polled on the sidewalk in front of the J. Press haberdashery store in New Haven, Conn. The question was: *Why did Washington cross the Delaware?*

70% gave evasive answers and said they were late for a squash game.

18% (all young lady students) said they were busy jacking up their consciousnesses and had no time to answer loaded questions about male jingoist porcine war-mongers and white slave traders.

7% demanded to know if this Washington was a Yale man before answering.

5% representing the college funny magazine got off comical answers such as "To get to the other side."

Now these students are not alone in their befuddlement. My own wife was Valedictorian of the Robinson Female Seminary in Exeter, New Hampshire, and she didn't know, either.

"From that picture," she said, "the boat seems to be heading west."

"How can you tell that?" I said.

"Boats heading from left to right are going east or north, right? Boats heading from right to left are going west or south, right?"

"I never thought of it that way. I guess you're right. That picture is misleading, they were going east."

"Well there you go," she said. "And why is Washington standing up in the boat like that? Hasn't he ever been in a rowboat before? Or does he think he's Douglas MacArthur? Another thing, look at the way that boat is overloaded. Look at the freeboard. And not a life jacket in sight. If the Coast Guard or the Harbor Police had come along about then they would have slapped a nice summons on him."

"Gee whiz honey I guess you're right," I said. "But don't you know where they were going?"

"Oh I suppose to Philadelphia or Bryn Mawr or Valley Forge or someplace."

"Damn it they weren't going west. They were going over to Trenton to crump the Hessians in a huge fantastic martial coup. Frederick the Great said it was the most brilliant maneuver in military history."

"What do you want for supper?" she said. "Or would you rather go out and eat Chinese?"

Washington didn't cross the Delaware in rowboats. You can't hardly get a lot of horses and 18 artillery pieces in rowboats. Besides, they had some fairly bulky officers for the excursion among the picturesque ice floes. Washington weighed in at 212 and Henry Knox at 280.

They used "Durham boats," the common freight carriers of the Delaware River. These were flat bottom double-ender keel boats from forty to sixty feet long. They were not rowed with oars like the lads in "the picture" who are having such a bad time. Beside the steersman they had a crew of four, who pushed these heavy craft forward with setting poles, sweating and shoving and cussing as they struggled on running boards from bow to stern. (These boats were also used on the Mohawk River and all the way up to the rivers of Ontario.)

Just 11 years later John Fitch's first steamboat made its trial run right here on the Delaware River. It made

7 miles an hour. Eventually humans would not have to
break their backs shoving cargo boats. But don't worry,
they would think of something else to grouse about.

"The picture" of "Washington Crossing the Delaware" was painted 60 years after the event and far
away in another land. Emmanuel Leutze was the cul-
prit. He committed this affront to the Museum of
Modern Art and Andrew Warhol at Düsseldorf, on
the Rhine. He obviously didn't do much homework
before he started laying on the burnt umber but it
doesn't matter. This chromo has such a heady effect
on otherwise rational people that a man in Omaha recently paid $260,000.00 for a *copy* of it by Eastman
Johnson. *Time* magazine says this is the highest price
ever paid at an auction by an American for an American painting.

So Washington crossed the Delaware and arrived at
Trenton in a snowstorm early in the A.M. of December 26th, 1776.

He captured the entire garrison of 1000 Hessians.
Oberstleutnant Rahl, commander of the detachment,
was slain.

It was the only American victory in history in which
all the prisoners, both officers and men, were found to
be suffering from severe heartburn and hangovers.

Battle of Trenton 1776

On Christmas day in seventy-six
Our ragged troops with bayonets fixed
   For Trenton marched away.
The Delaware see! the boats below!
The light obscured by hail and snow!
   But no signs of dismay.

Our object was the Hessian band
That dared invade fair freedom's land
   And quarter in that place.
Great Washington he led us on,
Whose streaming flag, in storm or sun,
   Had never known disgrace.

In silent march we passed the night,
Each soldier panting for the fight,
   Though quite benumbed with frost,
Greene, on the left, at six began,

The right was led by Sullivan,
  Who ne'er a moment lost.

Their pickets stormed, the alarm was spread
That rebels risen from the dead
  Were marching into town.
Some scampered here, some scampered there,
And some for action did prepare,
  But soon their arms laid down.

Twelve hundred servile miscreants,
With all their colors, guns and tents,
  Were trophies of the day.
The frolic o'er, the bright canteen
In centre, front and rear was seen
  Driving fatigue away.

Now, brothers of the patriot bands,
Let's sing deliverance from the hands
  Of arbitrary sway.
And as our life is but a span,
Let's touch the tankard while we can,
  In memory of that day.

☞ **ELEVEN** ☜

A FEW DAYS AFTER the fracas at Trenton, Washington went over and cleaned the kraut cohorts out of Princeton. They had been behaving in a perfectly beastly manner over there, pillaging, burning and even acting with "lust and brutality in abusing women."

When the Rebels arrived the mercenary vultures holed up in old Nassau Hall at the colledge and said "*Tausendmal nein*" when requested to surrender. An American cannonball was sent through the wall of the venerable seat of learning with a promise of more to come and the expeditionaries changed their minds *mit Eilfertigkeit*.

Washington went into headquarters at Morristown for the winter. The British had been booted out of central and western New Jersey.

It was the first "turning point of the war."

All the crabs who had been saying Washington was a flop and oughtta go back to fox hunting now did an about face and claimed he was the greatest thing since gunpowder. And they began writing gushy poems about him to the newspapers. Editors sailed over the cuckoo's nest:

"Washington retreats like a General and acts like a hero. If there are spots in his character, they are like the spots in the sun, only discernible by the magnifying powers of the telescope. Had he lived in the days of idolatry, he had been worshipped as a god."

After Trenton, Lord Howe, completely flummoxed by the news, refused to accept the fact that "three old established regiments of a people who make war a profession, should lay down their arms to a ragged and undisciplined militia."

The "ragged militia," as the British persisted in calling the American Continental Army, never ceased to amaze the aristocratic royalists, from Lexington to Yorktown. And they kept crying "Impossible" right to the very, very bitter end.

When the bad news from Princeton came on top of that from Trenton, Howe was so upset that when his mistress plumped herself on his Lordship's lap for a frolic he pleaded a sick headache, drank two bottles of Madeira, bawled out his aides-de-camp, and lay down on the sofa with a vinegar compress on his basilic brow.

1777.

It was called "The Gallows Year" because all those 777's looked like gibbets. Cheery notion.

It turned out to be a rotten year for George Washington. He lost Philadelphia and drew bad cards at Brandywine, Paoli, and Germantown and ended up at the devil's own winter quarters, Valley Forge.

Which he chose on purpose.

But far in the northland, amid the sylvan scenes of the headwaters of the Hudson, the American rabble in arms caused an entire British army to disappear.

It was the *second* "turning point of the war."

The vanishing British army was the result of the Battle of Saratoga, which is always included in those oppressive display volumes called "Fifteen Decisive Battles in History."

The cast of characters was unusual. The 18th Century was an era in which eccentricity and unbridled kookdom ran riot from the Court of Catherine of Russia, throughout Europe, and to the village explainers and domestic oddballs of New England.

A large force of troops under General John Burgoyne came down from Quebec and took Ticonderoga. These troops consisted of British and German regulars, Canadians and red Indians.

"Ticonderoga" was a pregnant and magic word in Whitehall, in the coffee shops and clubs of London, and also in the Colonies. It was the gateway to the Hudson River and New England, a key, a talisman, an American Gibraltar. It also sounded like a good 10 cent cigar.

When the news reached King George of the capture of Ticonderoga, he rushed into the Queen's parlor, where she was eating bread and Robertson's coarse cut Seville orange marmalade, and he cried "I have beat them! beat all the Americans!"

Horace Walpole, a brilliant fuddy-duddy who was never at a loss, remarked, "I hear Burgoyne has kicked Ticonderoga into one of the lakes — I don't know which — I am no geographer."

Burgoyne continued south through heavily wooded territory which had been laid waste by General John Schuyler. Schuyler was an aristocrat and also loaded. He had a mansion in Saratoga and another one in Albany. His wife was a Van Cortlandt and his mother a Van Rensselaer, enough to make him cordially disliked in New England. This distaste for and suspicion of New Yorkers has persisted in New England, especially in Boston, for nearly two centuries. (Cf.: *"The Late George Apley"* by the late John Marquand.)

Schuyler was a poor commander, never spoke to his troops, and was highly unpopular, but on this occasion he ravaged Burgoyne's line of march so thoroughly that the British engineers were able to move the army forward at a rate of only one mile per day.

Burgoyne's entourage for this junket in a hostile foreign wilderness beegles the boggles of the mind:

7400 fighting men. Seven thousand four hundred.

"Brave but dumb" German officers totally incapable of coping with "open order combat over broken terrain."

The unpalatable French-Canadian scoundrel Louis St. Luc de la Corne, in charge of 400 loot-happy Indians, who murdered the "beautiful" Tory maiden Jane McRae,* causing an uproar that ripped through the colonies, and aroused violent indignation in England.

Baroness von Riedesel, wife of German General von Riedesel, and her three small children, nursemaids, trunks, wardrobe, dishes and silverware, linens, beds, hair curlers, etc. She followed the caravan through the wilderness in a caleche — sort of like a Victorian dog cart.

Lady Harriet Acland, wife of Major Acland, son of Sir Thomas and his lady, daughter of Lord Ilchester, sister to the famous Lady Susan, etc. etc., with *her* baggage as above. She followed the action in a two wheel tumbril. Her husband the Major was shot through both legs and mortally wounded at Saratoga. She went through to the American side under a white flag to nurse him until he expired. American General Gates — called "Granny" by his troops because he wore

---

* I'm tellin' you fer the last time, Marlon. Lay that shootin' arn down or prepare to eat lead like it was piñon nuts.

spectacles and was a fuss pot — wrote to his wife —
whom Charles Lee referred to as a "Medusa" and "a
tragedy in private life, a farce to the world" — that
Lady Harriet was "the most amiable, delicate piece of
quality you ever beheld."

Then there was the great General Burgoyne and
General Burgoyne's personal necessities such as an ex-
tensive and complicated wardrobe, silver table service,
100 cases of champagne and a mistress who was fond
of late hours and the bubbly.

Over 500 women, many with children, plus an out-
rageous amount of excess baggage, and unnumbered
nondescript camp followers, trollops, bawds, strumpets, drabs and minxes, as well as dozens of pet dogs.

The supply train for this mixed bag of officers, soldiers, lady aristocrats, bums, and animals ran 125 miles
back to Montreal.

Figure if you will, as the French say, the plight of
the parade-ground foot soldiers from *Norddeutschland*
in the turbulent, scraggly forests and hills of unfriendly
rural New York State.

The British soldier carried sixty pounds of junk on
his back.

But lo, the poor dragoons from Woldenbuttel, Gau-
dersheim and Holzminden! They staggered under a
parody of military garb: huge seven-league jack boots,
stiff leather breeches, a hat drenched in feathers, enormous gauntlets — and besides carrying a heavy car-

bine, they each had a broadsword dangling off the hip weighing 12 pounds.

The weather was oppressively hot, sticky and stifling during the entire campaign.

The Americans were in their shirtsleeves. "Not one of them was properly uniformed," reported one of the Brunswick dragoons from under his ten pound hat, "but each man had on the clothes in which he goes to the field, to church, or to the tavern."

The Americans were also on their native soil while the opposition were 3000 miles from home, hearth, Mother and dear Phoebe or Frieda.

Such were the warriors who faced each other with stern resolution beside the halcyon Hudson in July, August and September of 1777.

Saratoga: Part Two

Horatio Gates was the victorious commander of the Continental forces. He has also been called a bungler, a weakling, an old woman, a marplot, a coward, a schemer, a ninny, a mooncalf, a plodder, a noddle, and a traitor to his commander-in-chief. After 200 years of historical pecking and rooting, he has emerged as the permanent and official whipping boy of the American Revolution.

Gates was an Englishman born. Very low born. We

wouldn't consider it low born, but we are not English. (My father was in trade, for example, but I am a member of the Elks Club in good standing.) His mother was a housekeeper for the Earl of Leeds. Dreadful. H. G. Wells's mother was a housekeeper and his father was a "professional cricketer." Dear me.

Due to the mother's connection with the house of Leeds, the aforementioned Horatio Horace Walpole agreed to be baby Gates's godfather, hence his name Horatio. He rose to the position of Major in the British army but his inability to rise in English society was a sore affliction.

In 1772, nose badly out of joint at a 35 degree angle, Gates decided to emigrate to the Colonies. He wrote George Washington, with whom he had served under Braddock at the Monongahela affair in '55, asking him about real estate in Virginia. He settled in Virginia on an estate which he called "Travellers Rest." Not very original, but still, not "Dunroamin" or "Journey's End."

When the Revoluton business began to boom he was in luck. To his amazement he was offered a commission as Brigadier General and became instanter the first Adjutant General of the American army. He was one of the very few American generals who had seen service in a regular army. He became a Major General in 1776.

Throughout his military career Gates preferred intrigue to "following the calfskin." (A military drum has a calfskin head.) He haunted the lobby of Congress and soon had more enemies in the colonies than King George himself.

Gates looked like Lon Chaney after six hours with the makeup man: long hooked nose, heavy features, lantern chin, droopy lids and small calculating eyes, not unlike those of the famed "Beadeye" Ryan.

He succeeded, by some underhanded finesse, in displacing General Schuyler as Commander-in-Chief of the Northern Department. Schuyler remained as a subordinate. Benedict Arnold arrived, and so did that tough nut Daniel Morgan with his riflemen, the most famous corps of the Continental Army.

After First Saratoga, Gates and Arnold were at each other's throats and Arnold was relieved of command and went and sat in his tent with a bottle of brandy.

During the second and final battle of Saratoga, Gates remained in his headquarters fully two miles away from the action. He could not even see what was going on by standing on a chair. Arnold erupted from quarantine and without orders hurled himself with Benedictine bravado, despite his old wound from Quebec, into the perilous fray. He and Schuyler won the battle, though no one could believe it, least of all Gentleman Johnny.

Old humbug Gates took all the bows and became an overnight sensation like Harry K. Thaw, Floyd Collins, & c.

Gates got so damn puffed up that he began to patronize George Washington. But three years later he was a bum again and getting the table next to the kitchen.

That's one of the specialties of Our Heritage: making Saints out of Nobodies and then pasting them in the eye with custard pies when we discover they have got feet of clay, or in some cases mud.

"Lieutenant General John Burgoyne of HIS MAJESTY'S ARMIES in America, Col. of the QUEEN'S REGIMENT in Light Dragoons, GOVERNOR of FORT WILLIAM in *North Britain*, REPRESENTATIVE in the *Commons* of Great Britain in PARLIAMENT, and COMMANDER of an Army and Fleet employed in an *Expedition* from CANADA" — such was the royal representative and most puissant chieftain of our enemies here on the battlefield called "Saratoga."

Legend says that John Burgoyne was a bastard.

Legend is wrong again. Burgoyne may have been a bit of a bastard but he was not illegitimate.

He was a lot of person all at one time and packed more moxie than an East Boston corner store.

He was not only a General of top grade in that holy of holies, the British Army, but he was a *playwright*. A playwright. A *successful* playwright.

Now can you imagine Dwight Eisenhower, Stonewall Jackson, Ulysses S. Grant or John Pershing writing a play and having it produced on Broadway? Burgoyne's play *The Maid of the Oaks* was produced by David Garrick in 1775. His comedy *The Heiress* appeared in 1786 and the printed version ran into ten editions within a year and was translated into several foreign languages making it very hard to pronounce.

He went to school at Westminster where he acquired an unfortunate lifelong addiction to quoting Latin. He eloped with Lady Charlotte Stanley, sixth daughter of the eleventh Earl of Derby. He gambled and gamboled. He wrote poetry. He was handsome, dashing and gay. After his wife's death (while he was on the Saratoga campaign) he "formed an attachment" with Susan Caulfield, an opera singer by whom he had several little Britons.

His soldiers called him "Gentleman Johnny" Burgoyne. They thought he was the nuts because he was the first officer in British military history possessed of the unique notion that foot soldiers were a branch of the human race. He actually talked to them and told them to write home to their mothers. He also fought alongside them.

He was quite a guy. (Cf. *Guy* Fawkes, 1570–1606). But he had another side.

Arthur Lee, our confidential agent in London, sent a report on him:

"A man of dark designs, deep dissimulations, desperate fortunes . . . engaged in every scene abhorrent from true religion and virtue . . ."

Tut, tut, Arthur. Let's try not to be sanctimonious.

Why did Burgoyne permit himself to be captured at Saratoga?

Because the whole plan of the campaign, hatched by that idiot Lord Germain, was crazy.

Instead of getting in deeper and deeper, why didn't he retreat?

He didn't retreat because Englishmen didn't retreat. Retreat would be weakness, unthinkable to a noble Briton of the 18th Century. Englishmen then spouted constantly of "reputation," "honor" and "fame." "Ambition" was another favorite. His ambition drove him into what was clearly a trap, and against hopeless odds. "Professional honor" was at stake. The entire surface of the globe is today littered with the skulls and bones of mortals who died for someone else's "professional honor."

Also he was rehearsing that familiar bit, the Englishman Abroad.

Speaking of this role in the world today, William Davis says in *Punch* of his countrymen:

"Abroad, they become more English than they ever were at home — just to make sure that no-one could possibly mistake them for anything else."

Burgoyne was infected with that sense of supercilious superiority to all other races and especially to gross, ill-bred, uncouth Americans.

After Saratoga, Burgoyne had the guts to say to

General Howe, "Had all my troops been British, I in my conscience believe I should have made my way through Mr. Gates's army."

Rule Britannia!

What went wrong, besides a supply train 125 miles long, dragging over 500 women in the van, etc., etc.?

Howe was supposed to come north and meet Burgoyne. Instead he went to Philadelphia.

St. Leger was supposed to come down the Mohawk valley and join Burgoyne. Instead, Benedict Arnold chased him out of Fort Stanwix and he hightailed it for Montreal.

Burgoyne sent 1500 men to Bennington, Vermont, to scare up some food, cattle, Granola grits and Tory recruits. Twenty-three Bennington Girls from the college came out and read their Honors Theses at the approaching British troops. 200 soldiers fell down dead, 700 were captured, and the rest retreated in disorder suffering brain fever.

Burgoyne was supposed to walk over the Continental army and eat Christmas dinner in Albany. He did have Christmas dinner in Albany — at General Schuyler's house — as a prisoner.

The British lost:

Two lieutenant generals, two major generals, three brigadiers, 299 other officers, 389 non-commissioned officers, 197 musicians, and 4836 privates.

Also 27 artillery pieces, 5000 stand of small arms, ammunition, gobs of military stores and an outlandish assortment of other impedimenta and combustibles.

Who got the drabs, trollops, strumpets, etc., I can't say. They are not mentioned in the ARTICLES OF CONVENTION, signed on the 17th of October 1777.

General Gates wrote to his wife, (the Medusa):

"If Old England is not by this lesson taught humility, then she is an old Slut, bent upon her ruin."

Totally Useless Facts

Last Surviving Patriot General, Thomas Sumter, d. 1832, age 98.

Last Land Battle: George Rogers Clark at Chillicothe, Ohio.

Youngest U. S. Commissioned Officer: Ensign Robert Wilson, 18 years old, of the New York Brigade. He accepted the battle flags from the defeated British at Yorktown.

Number of Americans who served in the Army: 230,000.

Number of Militia ditto: 56,000.

Number of Veterans on Pension List in 1867: 2.

Martha Dandridge Custis's dowry: 15,000 acres of land near Williamsburg; $65,000 cash in the bank; 150 slaves.

John Paul Jones's employment after the war: Rear-Admiral in the Russian navy.

General Howe's pet dog got lost in the fog at the

Battle of Germantown and General Washington sent him back to his owner under a flag of truce.

There were four Georgian Kings in the years 1714–1830.

In April 1973 there were 42,000 troops engaged in "war exercises" on the North Carolina coast.

George Washington as a young man wrote terrible love poems.

 **TWELVE**

Sunday, April 6, 1975

Ate breakfast at Zinn's Diner on route 222 Denver, Pa., Exit 21 Penna Turnpike. This is one of those *komisch* Pennsylvania Dutch joints where the menu offers "Pork mit Kraut," "Chicken und Waffles," etc. George Washington once stopped here and was offered "Beef Heart mit Filling." We had a good breakfast with plenty "mit" and side orders of "und."

Arr. Valley Forge in pouring rain. "Reception Center" and museum. Usual flintlocks, shoe buckles, uniforms — also von Steuben's Deutsch-Englisch dictionary, Lady Stirling's reticule and facsimile bloody footprints in plaster casts.

For $5.25 (one month's pay for a private in the Continental Army) we rented the OFFICIAL tape tour recording gadget which would "recreate in living sound" (rather than in "dead sound" or "silence") "the real meaning of Valley Forge." It would "come alive" faster than the girl could make change.

So we got in the car and after eating two doughnuts purchased yesterday at Do-Nut Heaven in Greensboro, N. C., not far from Guilford Court House, we consulted the handy FREE map and began the tour. The real meaning of Valley Forge and Our American Heritage came alive instantly.

In order to keep kids and their dull-witted parents awake, and to make it more "meaningful" the story is told in the first person by a supposed private in the Colonial Army. Inspiration is plentiful but information is sub-zero.

This private has an Actor's School idea of a 1777 American soldier's voice, i. e., gutsy, colloquial, with overtones of Steve McQueen.

Among other choice bits, this 18th Century soldier in George Washington's army says ". . . meanwhile Cornwallis is having a ball in Philadelphia . . ." ". . . the big brass . . ." and "those guys have it made." Any minute I expected him to say "Like man, y'know, this Valley Forge is way out, y'know."

This script is a "Freedoms Foundation Awards Winner," Manny, and I see a very big picture here if we can just inject a little hangy-pangy some kind with Martha Washington and like some good lookin' Redford-type young lonesome lieutenant, not enough nobody takes offense y'unnerstand.

There is not much left here at the Forge. A few replica huts. It began to snow so M. took my picture in front of a brummagem hut in the snow.

The place is big. I thought it would be about the size of Union Square. Actually it wanders all over up slopes and down dales and has so many roads snaking around and crisscrossing that you get lost and keep arriving back at the simulated blacksmith shop again, near the facsimile Rest Rooms.

Strange to say, there is no carbon copy of the original iron foundry.

Lunched at the "George Washington Motor Lodge" which is only minutes away from the Forge and features a "special golf and theatre package," "Gourmet dining" (don't get excited, they are now selling "gourmet" chili-mac on South State St. in Chi.) and banquet and convention facilities for the Big Brass from Pottstown, Monocacy and Allentown.

"It was such a depressing war. Eight years! I don't know how Washington stood it," says M.

"By September 1777," I replied, "Washington had banished Madeira from his table and was serving rum and water."

"Poor dear," she said.

Got gas at King of Prussia. You can't beat that for the name of a town. I suppose it has something to do with that jolly old faker von Steuben . . .

If Valley Forge hadn't happened, the National Guild of Patriotic Speech Writers (founded 1783) would have had to invent it.

"December 18, 1777. Continental Army camps at Valley Forge, where naked, starving, unpaid troops suffer terrible hardships but survive."

Why did Washington pick this place anyway?

That other amiable hoax, "Baron" de Kalb, son of a German peasant, a Major General in the American Army, said this site could only have been selected "at the instance of a speculator, or on the advice of a traitor, or by a council of ignoramusses " (*Unwissendeversammlung*).

General Varnum, from Thoreau's precious Merrimack River Country, waxed wroth.

"It is unparalleled in the history of mankind to establish winter quarters in a country wasted and without a single magazine."

This did not mean that the army had no supply of back issues of the *National Geographic* and *True Detective*. A magazine is a warehouse full of military supplies and Spam, wool sox, Hershey bars, blankets and Climax Cut Plug chewing tobacco.

No magazines had been prepared in the neighborhood and the camp was plunk in the middle of a nest of horrid Tory farmers who naturally preferred to sell their fresh eggs, country butter, and fat porkers to Howe, twenty miles away in Philadelphia.

Washington did everything but grovel to the Continental Congress for help. They responded in characteristic fashion by immediately ordering 10,000 pairs of shoes for the shivering lads — from France. These shoes arrived in 1785, two years after the Peace Treaty, and were sold to Army Surplus stores for 12¢ a pair.

Transport was the main problem. There was plenty of stuff in the other colonies but there was no Pennsylvania Railroad, no Ryder trucks, no United Parcel Delivery.

And prices were a crime. The war profiteers were doing big business at the old stand. A soldier could buy a pair of shoes in the spring of 1776 for eight shillings. By the winter of 1777 the cost was up to eight dollars. Before long it would be one hundred dollars.

General Henry Knox left Valley Forge in midwinter to go to Boston to purchase anti-shivering goods for the troops. He also wanted to see his wife Lucy (née Flucker) but he didn't tell G. W. that. He didn't fool George none. Anyway the patriotic Boston yankees put the gouge on him so bad that he came back to the foundry without placing a single order. (However he did bring Lucy Knox, formerly Lucy Flucker, with him, and she joined Martha Washington and her lady friends in their daily hen parties and sewing bees. She was a live wire and came in loud and clear. Both Lucy, daughter of a Boston Flucker, and her husband the General "had the lovable joviality typical of fat people and it rubbed off on others.")

Another factor causing distress to the army was the apathy of at least one half of the non-Tory colonists. "They couldn't care less," as the writers for the Freedoms Foundation would put it with acerb originality.

Things were really bad.

Surgeon Albigence (sic) Waldo, of the Connecticut Line:

"It snows — I'm sick — eat nothing — no whiskey — no forage — Lord — Lord — Lord . . . discontented — and out of humor. Poor food — hard lodging — cold weather — fatigue — nasty cloathes — nasty cookery — vomit half my time — smoaked out of my senses — the devil's in't — I can't endure it. Why are we sent here to starve and freeze? — What sweet felicities have I left at home: a charming wife — pretty children — good beds — good food — good cookery — all agreeable — all harmonious! Here all confusion — smoke and cold — hunger and filthyness — a pox on my bad luck! There comes a bowl of beef soup full of leaves and dirt, sickish enough to make a Hector spue — away with it, boys! I'll live like the chameleon upon air.

"What have you for your dinners, boys? 'Nothing but fire cake and water Sir.' At night: 'Gentlemen, the supper is ready.' What is your supper, lads? 'Fire cake and water, Sir.' "

Fire-cake was flour-and-water paste baked in thin cakes on hot stones. In other words, *crackers.*

When the unhappy surgeon said he was "smoked out of his senses" he didn't mean that he had got up to three packs of Camels a day. The men lived twelve in a 14 x 16 foot hut with a fireplace in the end made of wood and clay. They had nothing but green wood to burn and it smoked like hell.

". . . lay Cold and uncomfortable last Night," says Dr. Waldo, "my eyes are started out from their Orbits like a Rabbit's eyes, occasion'd by a great Cold & smoke . . .

". . . The Lord send that our Commissary of Purchases may live on Fire Cake & Water, 'till their glutted Gutts are turned to Pasteboard."

And yet, the diaries are not all bitching and moaning. The boys had their jokes, which they no doubt ran into the ground.

"Good morning brother soldier, how are you?"

"All wet, thank 'e. Hope you're so."

And General Knox's biographer says (please don't let the D. A. R. hear of this) that many men at Valley Forge ran loose and took to "pillaging, drinking, and running after women."

The winter was not as cold as the following winter in Morristown which was a baster. But it sufficed. It served the purpose. Up north the ice in New York harbor froze so solid that the British hauled heavy cannon across on it from Staten Island to Manhattan.

The second week in February was a bad one. It snowed so hard no wagons could get to the camp so rations were reduced from flour paste to nothing.

A thieving lieutenant was to have had his sword broken over his head publicly. But the snow fell so thick and fast that General Washington called the game due to snow.

The third week in February was even worse.

But on February 23rd of '78, while the acrid smoke from the fires of green wood filled the air, a wondrous apparition appeared before the amazed eyes of the scarecrow army. It seemed to be human. Though it spoke no English it was immensely cheerful. It was garbed in a glorious uniform of scarlet and gold. On its breast was an astonishing military decoration, a star as big as a soup plate.

It was called Baron Friedrich Wilhelm Augustus Heinrich Ferdinand von Steuben, aide-de-Camp of Frederick the Great, Lieutenant General in the King of Prussia's service, Grand Marshal at the court of the Prince of Hohenzollern-Hechingen, and Grand Marshal at the court of the Margrave of Baden. That's what it was called.

But what it really was, was good old Fritz Steuben, son of a poor Lutheran pastor, who after years in the Prussian army had risen no higher than captain. The rest was fantasy. The soup plate decoration could have been a reward for Prevarication Beyond the Call of

Duty, for the Baron was a most magnificent and cheerful liar.

Von Steuben had offered his services and Congress had voted its thanks to the forty-seven-year-old, penniless soldier of fortune ("illustrious stranger") and turned him over to Washington.

Washington groaned. Not *another* medal-encrusted foreign soldier wanting to play war with the Americans at the rank and pay of a General! Washington groaned several more times.

"Get rid of him, Lafayette old chap, will you?" he said.

But . . .

"No other foreign soldier," says Douglas Southall Freeman, "except Lafayette and perhaps the engineer Duportail, so quickly won a place in the esteem of the Army."

Henry Laurens reported to an absent member of Congress who was home mending fences, collecting rebates and selling Army commissions, etc., that the bogus Generalissimo "has hit the taste of the officers, gives universal satisfaction and has made an amazing improvement in discipline."

Von Steuben was a Tony Award actor, but he was an even better drill master. He introduced "uniform and expeditious maneuver." He cancelled hay-foot, straw-foot, and soon had our boys marching and drilling according to the latest European styles. He changed the step. He got right out with the boys and acted as drill sergeant. He even made the lads like it.

He knew no English and did all this in French, through French-speaking Captain Ben Walker. His inability to swear in English frustrated him on occasion, so he called on Walker:

"*Viens* Walker, *mon ami, mon bon ami! sacré!* Goddam de *gaucheries* of dese *badauts! Je ne puis plus. Merde!* Can't curse dem no good."

The old boy psyched them up and soon had the scarecrows proud of their rags and tatters. Officers began to chuckle and flaunt their worn-out britches. They say he coined the word *sansculottes* right here at Valley Forge, even though he got no royalties for it from the French Revolution. Anyway it made a big hit with the Army at Valley Forge and the boys said, "Say, the Baron is all right."

Everything picked up after von Steuben got there and the officers began to have little parties. "Spartan entertainment" began at Washington's stone house down by the creek, Martha being assisted by Mrs. Nathanael Greene, Lucy F. Knox, Lady Stirling, Lady Kitty Stirling, and other lovely tomatoes.

And soon it was spring, robins cackled in the gorse, and France came in on our side against King George and the power of Great Britain. And a good thing too. We'd never of made it without them.

So the American people, who have always detested the French (and vice versa) now screamed with joy at the alliance, in spite of "French morals," the cancan, absurd speech, eating snails and peeing in public.

The troops lined up and under direction of the Chief they all shouted, "Huzza for the King of France!"

This was followed by a grand military review during which Madame Nathanael Greene chatted in schoolgirl French with the affable Baron, expressing sentiments with regard to her aunt's pen and the door being both open and closed. Von Steuben made casual reference to "my estates in Swabia," which existed only in the puffball of his imagination.

At the close of the display a cold collation was served up and George Washington's glacial mien suffered a temporary thaw as he "played cricket with the Junior officers."

A British spy who had watched the new von Steubenish military precision displayed by the troops was caught lurking behind the punch bowl. Instead of being hanged from the nearest sweet gum tree he was turned loose with instructions to go back and tell Sir Billy Howe all about it.

If he did, Lord Howe must have yawned, for his resignation as miss-the-boat Commander-in-Chief had been speedily accepted back on the shores of the Thames.

He was succeeded in Philadelphia by Sir Henry Clinton, who proceeded to evacuate the cradle of liberty on June 18, 1778. He left behind an extremely putrid cradle.

The omnipresent General Henry Knox rushed into town from Valley Forge.

"Lucy and I went in," he said, "but it stunk so abominably that it was impossible to stay there, as was her first design."

George Washington Doing a Nixon on the "Media"

Jefferson wrote to Madison that President Washington was "extremely affected by the attacks made and kept up on him in the public papers. I think he feels these things more than any person I ever met with."

The Secretary of State noted that, at a cabinet meeting "Presid't Washington was much inflamed, got into one of those passions when he cannot command himself, ran on much about the personal abuse which had been bestowed on him . . . that *by god* he had rather be in his grave than in his present situation. That he had rather be on his farm than to be made *emperor of the world* and yet that they were charging him with wanting to be a king. That that *rascal Freneau* sent him 3 of his papers every day, as if he thought he would become the distributor of his papers, that he could see in this nothing but an impudent design to insult him . . ."

He also complained about "the abuse of Mr. Bache" (editor of the *Aurora*) and his correspondents and deplored "with what malignant industry and persevering falsehoods I am assailed in the *Aurora* of this city."

When George Washington retired to Mt. Vernon from the Presidency he cut off all newspaper subscriptions. But evidently this resolve collapsed because on the night of his last illness he read the papers until after nine o'clock, and "when he met with anything he thought diverting or interesting, he would read it aloud as well as his hoarseness would permit."

And Thomas Jefferson, no doubt referring to the Washington *Post*, the New York *Times*, the Chicago *Tribune*, the St. Louis *Post-Dispatch* and the Manchester (N.H.) *Leader*, said:

"The man who reads nothing at all is better educated than the man who reads nothing but newspapers."

Or as Adolphe Menjou said in *The Front Page:*
"The son of a bitch stole my watch!"

☞ THIRTEEN ☜

ALL THE JADES, whores, and trulls from far and wide, possibly even some from the shambles of Saratoga, had swarmed into Philadelphia after the British occupation. Disease, debauchery, desertion and high jinks took their toll.

Lord Howe and Mrs. Loring (called "The Sultana" by the British Army) were still at it hammer and tongs. And he had the faro table, the Walnut Street Theatre and the dancing assembly, all of which were more to his taste than the inconveniences of camp and cannon and the bother of pursuing an enemy, shooting guns, wet feet, etc.

So he went back to England to do some explaining (did The Sultana go with him? I don't know) and Sir Henry Clinton pulled stakes for New York, abandoning Philadelphia forever.

On the way Washington started a fight with Clinton at Monmouth, New Jersey. Eccentric, possibly traitorous Major General Charles Lee, who led the advance attack, ordered a retreat. He ran headlong into Washington, who gave him the Bessemer eye and a piece of his mind in shrapnel form.

The temperature at the height of the battle was 96°. The British suffered 358 casualities, 58 being from sunstroke. Americans 360 dead, 40 of sunstroke.

Clinton proceeded to New York. Washington went to Haverstraw. Both armies were now back where they had been two years before.

General Charles Lee was courtmartialled on several charges and deprived of command for one year. A few months later this strange man decided to write an insulting letter to Congress. They tossed him out on his ear for good.

The Continental Army, in fighting trim from the fresh air and invigorating daily drill at Valley Forge, was raring to go. But they didn't go noplace in 1778.

Nor in 1779.

Nor in 1780.

General Clinton held New York. His position was impregnable. George Washington and the Republican army were equally inexpugnable at West Point, where they lurked behind chevaux-de-frises, fireboats, chains, gunboats, abatis, flèches, demilunes, ravelins, redans and redoubts.

For three glum years these two armies maintained this boring scenario.

The big news of 1778 was that George Rogers Clark took Kaskaskia, out on the Mississippi River. Then he went over to Cahokia, another British outpost about as big as a minute, and took that. But the big deal was Vincennes, on the Wabash.

Up in the British fort at Detroit there was a particularly unsavoury commander, Lieutenant Colonel Henry Hamilton, called "The Hair Buyer." He provided the local Indians with 8,640 scalping knives, and other nice gifts, and when they brought in the scalps of American men, women, and children this brave minion of King George added lustre to the glory of British arms by giving them more gifts.

This fine gentleman rushed down to Vincennes to hold the fort there — Fort Sackville. He settled in for the winter and figured he was all right because it was December, the weather was a fright, plus all the streams for miles around were flooded out of their banks. Clark could not possibly get through those frozen swamps and icewater streams. Hamilton resumed passing out favors to the Indians: more scalping knives.

George Rogers Clark, who used his middle name, decided that this would be a good time to become a National Hero so he made an "impossible" march of 180 miles through above noted frigid floods, staggered into Vincennes, and sacked Fort Sackville.

Lieutenant Colonel Hamilton and G. R. Clark met after the capitulation to discuss terms. The Englishman complained that Clark was being too rough on him.

Clark did not mince up his words. This was no parade ground parley with flags, suitable for framing.

"Could I look on you Sir as a Gentleman I would do the utmost of my power, but on you Sir who have embrued your hands in the blood of our women and children — honor, my country, everything calls on me alloud for Vengeance."

The charming "Hair Buyer" was sent off clanking with chains to the Williamsburg jail house.

The United States now controlled the Ohio-Indiana-Illinois country and continued to do so. This was the greatest conquest of territory during the whole war and was accomplished with an "army" of 175 men.

In the Peace Treaty of 1783 Britain turned over to us an "inland empire comprising the present extent of the five largest mid-western states." All as a result of George Rogers Clark.

"Never since Cortez and Clive had so few men made such a mark on history."

And never in history have the legislative bodies of his government heaped such smuts on a hero in his lifetime.

Clark had financed the expedition out of his own pocket and from personal loans. He asked the Virginia legislature, who had approved the expedition, if they would please reimburse him for his trouble as he was completely broke.

This solemn body of patriots went into deep thought and pondered for several years with no result.

People he had borrowed money from to pay for his men's wages, supplies, and food began to sue him. Even the Wabash Land Company — if you like irony help yourself to that.

Clark petitioned the Continental Congress, who had also authorized the campaign, for some lagniappe seeing as how he had handed them several billion acres of the finest land on the globe.

The Congress issued most amazing high velocity gusts of patriotic wind and then, exhausted from the effort, voted themselves a raise in pay and retired to the Turkish baths.

Clark retired destitute and remained in this unenviable condition for a hero until he died in 1818, a pauper.

In his old age, after the Virginia legislature had thought it over for some thirty years, they finally decided to reward George Rogers Clark, native son and hero of Kaskaskia and Vincennes.

They sent him a sword, which cost them $22.50 with the discount, as one of the supreme legislators had a brother-in-law who owned a sword factory.

Since Clark died in 1818 the Federal and State governments have spent 2.4 million dollars on monuments in his honor.

"The George Rogers Clark Memorial is the largest national monument of its kind west of Washington, D.C. A magnificently proportioned pillared rotunda of white marble and Indiana limestone in which Clark stands in bronze surrounded by murals . . . it is as imposing as the Lincoln Memorial and as tranquil as the Jefferson." (New York *Times*)

When they presented him with the sword he said "I want bread, not toys."

Sleep well, George, things haven't changed a damn bit.

During the rest of 1778 there was a great deal of nastiness in Pennsylvania and New York. We will draw the veil on the massacre at Wyoming Valley by the infamous Butler with 1600 Tories and Indians who "memorized another Golgotha" (Shakespeare) both here and at Cherry Valley. Suffice it to say that wanton destruction and cruelty chilled the blood. Even the superheated blood of other British officers, who saw nothing but humiliation to British honor in such interesting exercises as locking up women and children in their houses and burning them up.

"The honor and Grandeur of Great Britain were never in a more despicable situation than the present owing entirely to the misconduct of the Villainous Minority [Tories] and I hope in God if the Army is obliged to leave America that the first thing they will do when they land in Britain is to Scalp every son of a Bitch of them."

Thus spoke British Captain Alexander McDonald of his co-warriors.

The war moved to the South, which was filled with loyalists foaming at the mouth. In Georgia and the Carolinas it turned into a vicious civil war of guerilla raids, malicious destruction and plain murder.

Benedict Arnold said his leg wound from Saratoga was giving him a bad time and asked General Washington if he could have the command at Philadelphia which would require no leaping about on horses and waving swords. His petition was granted. Within days he was up to his soon-to-be-traitorous neck in the black market and branched out to selling army supplies at which he made a killing. Washington was evidently too innocent to inquire how come, on a salary of $332 a month in rubber Continental money, Arnold suddenly blossomed out with a stately mansion, a coach and four, and liveried servants. Presently he had sufficiently dazzled eighteen-year-old Tory society belle Peggy Shippen with his social magnificence. She married him. They made a perfect pair.

Two freaks.

Also in 1778 Sir John Dalrymple suggested that George Washington be offered a dukedom "and revenue to support it" if he would give up the General business and go back to fox hunting, possibly in England.

The year ended with the Capture of the port of Savannah, Georgia, by the British. The defense by General Robert Howe was a masterpiece of bungledom and the whole state of Georgia was lost, which of course embraced John Styth Pemberton's Coca-Cola factory at 107 Marietta Street in Atlanta.

Did General Washington Swear at General Charles Lee at the Battle of Monmouth?

Yes, sir, he swore on that day till the leaves shook on the trees, charming, delightfully. Never have I enjoyed such swearing before or since. Sir, on that memorable day he swore like an angel from Heaven.

GENERAL CHARLES SCOTT

☞ **FOURTEEN** ☜

1779 wasn't much better.

January, February, and March winter quarters at Morristown made the previous winter at Valley Forge seem like a Sunday School picnic at Eagle Point Park.

The British failed to take Charleston.

The Rebels failed to take Savannah.

The might of Great Britain overcame the village of Fairfield, Connecticut, and robbed all the women of their "buckles, rings, bonnets, aprons, and handkerchiefs . . ."

British General Tryon rose to heights of military grandeur by sacking and burning the magnificent metropolis of Norwalk, Connecticut. On this occasion His Majesty's fearless warriors vanquished a local cooper called Deaf Fountain Smith who was taking a morning stroll in his garden. He was belted on the head and dumped in a prison in New York to die aetat fifty-four.

George Washington complained of inflation and said ". . . six or seven thousand pounds which I have in Bonds upon Interest is now reduced to as many hundreds . . ."

The Pennsylvania Council caught up with Benedict Arnold's profiteering and brought charges. The Army and the Continental Congress tried to cover up for him. Lack a day.

Washington went to Philadelphia and nearly danced all night with Mrs. Bache, Ben Franklin's daughter. He then returned to his H. Q. in Middlebrook, N. J. just in time for a slippery shoe jamboree. General Washington opened the ball with Guess Who? Lucy F— Knox, and the war-weary revelers danced all night.

It was that kind of a year.

Mad Dogs and Englishmen

These English are mad; they march through a country and think they have conquered it.

MARQUIS DE LAFAYETTE

☞ FIFTEEN ☜

DRAMAWISE the year 1779 laid an egg.

But in 1780 several productions were big box office.

In May the British grabbed Charleston, S. C., and everything in it. Among other things it contained was our entire glorious southern army.

Twenty-four days later came Tarleton's meat market at Waxhaw Creek, a day which will live in infamy along with a thousand others.

And again in July, although I see by the papers that we have never lost a war, a battle or a General's laundry, we took a creaming at Camden, S. C., during which another army was wiped out and our Fearless Leader Gates left the field and ran for two days.

Then in September — Sensation! Throw out that front page! Major André was captured with his boots stuffed with dynamite. Benedict Arnold rowed down the river, changed uniforms and became a General in the British Army. André was hanged, although nobody wanted it because he was a very neat guy. But war is a sorry business and spies must dance upon the air.

To make things worse, back in New Jersey Lucy Knox was knoxed up and couldn't dance.

But in October, while on a Fall Foliage Tour sponsored by the Chamber of Commerce, 1400 very ornery patriot mountaineers came upon a bunch of Tories on a Bird Watchers outing on Kings Mountain, North Carolina. In the discussion that followed the Tories were seized with lead poisoning and 300 of them fell dead.

This incident was received with enthusiasm in rebel quarters throughout the colonies, who had feared that The End Was Near and that cricket would soon be the official national pastime.

Sir Henry Clinton planned the investment of Charleston and was so serious about it that he actually left New York City and its Babylonian charms to come down in person. With a big fleet and 10,000 soldiers sailors and marines.

A siege was a textbook affair to professional Europeans, and Clinton meant business this time — no more funny stuff like in June of '76 when Admiral Parker lost his pants — and he played out the gambol by the book. The book called for the following moves in a siege:

First the harbor was blockaded and the city partially surrounded.

Second a long trench with gun batteries was made parallel to the fortifications of the city. This was the First Parallel.

Then under cover of the First Parallel zigzag trenches were dug by sappers, fanning out forward to a suitable point where the doughty diggers grubbed out and fortified the Second Parallel.

All this time, and it took weeks of shovel and spade work, there was more or less continual exchange of gunfire between besiegers and besieged making for noisy and dangerous working conditions.

From the Second Parallel the military moles burrowed out another labyrinth of trenches until they were within musket shot of the defenders.

Here they built the Third Parallel, manned it, set off a hell of a bombardment and called upon the garrison to throw in the towel.

If the legions behind the ramparts refused, then the offense settled down to starving them out, with a daily musical accompaniment in the lower registers from cannon hurling heavy round metallic lumps at the fortifications and over them into the city and the lobby of the Planters Hotel. (At the siege of Syracuse, we hear that Archimedes made hurling machines which threw stones at the foe weighing 1800 pounds.)

This was the classical method, approved by Philip

of Macedon and Sebastien le Prestre de Vauban, marshal of France and *ingénieur du roi*.

Sir Harry went through all this methodically, most
of the sapping work being done by his six regiments
of Germans who were doing a great job in the mole
dept. Not without some complaint. One officer mole
wrote home to *Mutter* grousing about "the confounded
pride and arrogant bearing of the English, who treat
everyone that was not born on their ragamuffin (*zer-
lumptig?*) Island with contempt."

Anyway about the time the sauerkraut sappers were
constructing the Second Parallel the British Fleet which
had been lurking out in the roadstead sailed over the
bar, right past Fort Moultrie and into town.

George Washington gave up when he heard of this
from afar and said, "The propriety of defending the
town depended on the probability of defending the
bar."

But the rebels, under General Benjamin Lincoln,
refused to wave the bedsheet, very foolishly, and the
siege went on for 33 more days of unpleasantness and
bedlam.

The jig made its appearance on April 24th when Sir
Henry began his Third Parallel and it was up on May
4th. The garrison surrendered with its battered mixture
of 6000 military and civilians.

The only American army in the South, including
the entire proud Virginia line, was now in chains.

Several days later a powder magazine containing 5000 captured muskets blew up, killing 40 redcoats and destroying the town whorehouse.

Shortly after the fall of Charleston began a period of horrors in the South.

Every so often in the annals of war a disciple of Beelzebub rears his vampire's head thirsting for gore. Such a monster had appeared in British raiment to bring eternal shame to the uniform and to the name of old England.

Colonel Banastre Tarleton, a product of Liverpool and Oxford University, was a butcher.

At Waxhaw Creek on May 28th, 1780, under pretext of a white flag, he slaughtered 113 patriots and left 150 still living but hacked to pieces on the field with no medical aid whatsoever.

It was here that the phrase "Tarleton's quarter" was born, meaning the massacre of defenseless men, men who had thrown down their arms and asked for "quarter."

Lord Cornwallis reported this sickening example of blood lust to the King as a jolly good show and said that Tarleton had the right stuff in him.

This was followed by a systematic plundering and looting of the South by the British. They stole everything in sight. They were not averse to stealing human bodies and in one shipment consigned 2000 negro slaves to the West Indies.

Grisly encounters between patriots and loyalists took place. This raw hatred between native born Americans was like madness. Nothing approaching it was ever seen during the War Between the States. And its only counterpart today exists at the Harvard-Dartmouth football game.

A new American army was slowly heading south under General Horatio ("Granny") Gates, the "hero of Saratoga," who now blundered into a catastrophe. Refusing any advice old Granny took off through a no man's land devoid of any comfort or forage. The boys came down with dysentery from eating the only things they could find, green corn and unripe peaches.

Colonel Lord Francis Rawdon (another unpleasant type) and Cornwallis were waiting for them at Camden, S. C. Gates bumbled on and the two armies collided in the middle of the hot sticky hungry summer night of August 15–16, 1780.

The next day they held a battle.

The Virginia militia threw down their guns and took to their heels, breaking several track records.

The North Carolina militia did likewise.

900 Continentals were now left on the field against the entire British army of 2250 men.

Our brave lads fought it out. They were squashed after prodigies of valor, and noble Major General Baron de Kalb, unhorsed, fighting fiercely with eleven wounds, fell here in the ghastly pine barrens of North America.

Some kindly British dragoons propped him up against a wagon, the better to strip him of his gold-laced coat. Cornwallis came along in time to discourage these attentions and had him moved to Camden. Despite the best care he died three days later, not for his country but for ours, a real hero, with a town in Illinois soon to be named for him, 60 miles west of Chicago, and the birthplace of barbed wire.

General Horatio Gates got on his horse immediately when the militia ran away, turned his back on the argument and sprinted for open space, not stopping until he reached Charlotte, *sixty miles from the battlefield.*

Although Gates was the slowest mover in our military chronicles, he had the fastest horse. In fact a race-horse — "the son of Colonel Baylor's 'Fearnaught,' own brother to His Grace of Kingston's famous 'Careless.'"

He got up early the next day and kept on running until he got to Hillsborough.

"Was there ever an instance of a general running away as Gates has done from his whole army?" Alexander Hamilton asked a friend. "And was there ever so precipitous a flight? One hundred and eighty miles in three days and a half! It does admirable credit to the activity of a man of his age . . ."

General Nathanael Greene, who replaced him, said ". . . you was unfortunate but not blameable."

Well that's a polite way of putting it. But it was the end of Gates.

Then when Americans were staring at the dregs of two horrible defeats in the bottoms of their pewter tankards (now worth $285.00 apiece), another blow fell and it was a block buster.

Hanging King George in effigy had been great sport in 1775 and 1776 but like all fads it had had its day. The facts of war had proved a good deal more dreary than all those fun protest meetings and nobody had been to a good effigy-hanging party in four years.

Now they had a new candidate and all the wahoos were soon out in the town square hanging effigies from telephone poles with all their former zest.

Lord Clinton had offered Arnold ten thousand pounds sterling to deliver West Point to him on a platter. This was a Fortune in far off 1780. That is why Benedict Arnold turned traitor.

And if Major André hadn't bungled, the plan would have gone through. As it was, Benedict Arnold received £6,315 plus a General's commission and pay, pensions, fringe benefits, discounts at the factory store and medical insurance.

Martha suggested to George that Arnold might suffer remorse.

"He is so hackneyed in Villainy," said George, as a statuesque figure in flowing robes labelled "Truth" removed a bandage from his eyes, "and so lost to all sense

of honor and shame, that while his faculties will enable
him to continue his sordid pursuits there will be no
time for remorse."

But there was.

Before he died in England in 1801 Benedict Arnold
cast aside his British scarlet and gold and asked for his
old American uniform, his "old blue and buff one." In
his diary he wrote "It is the only uniform I have ever
worn with honor and I would be buried in it."

When his man servant Sage found him he was dead
across the bed. He had got on his old coat and had
managed to get his lame leg from Quebec and Saratoga into one leg of the buff breeches. And so he died.

After becoming a British officer he had some sort
of a psychological seizure and attempted to outdo
bloody Banastre Tarleton. He butchered the garrison
at Fort Griswold in Groton, Connecticut, and sacked
and burned the town.

This was his native state, and his home town of Nor-
wich was only a few miles up the Thames river.

Then in October the Patriots fought Tories at Kings
Mountain, N. C., and won a victory that went thun-
dering up and down the land. It was Civil War. The
only Briton in the fight was the Tory leader, a fine
gentleman named Major Patrick Ferguson. The hellish
conduct of his British brethren in arms in the South
turned his stomach. Instead of burning houses and
shoving women around he went into rebel kitchens,

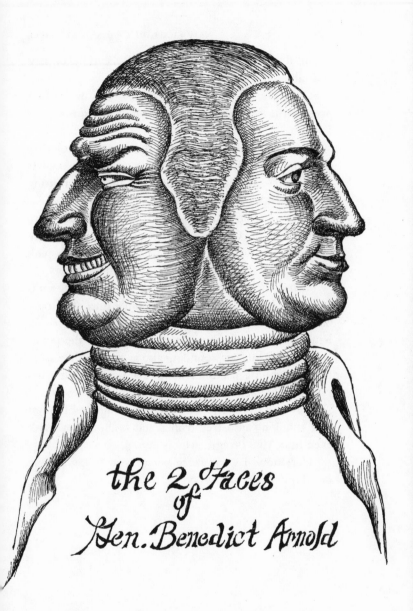

the 2 Faces
of
Gen. Benedict Arnold

bounced babies on his knee, passed the time of day and talked it over.

Somebody up at the Big Control Board in the Sky pushed the wrong button and Major Ferguson was killed.

It's a beautiful battleground, if that's not a contradiction, especially on a spring day with the violets under foot and the white dogwood blossoms floating up the hillsides and down into the glens.

There is a busload of 5th Grade schoolkids here from over in Gastonia, or maybe Belmont. Rosy cheeked lads with bubble gum cards, girls with pink knees and Crackerjack prize rings on their fingers.

Their fathers and mothers work in the hosiery mills and the chenille mills and the bombazine, buckram, burlap, batiste and braid mills, and these kids here on Kings Mountain in the pale spring speak in the popular Hee Haw accent, sounding also as though they were performers in a heart-warming TV series about true-blue rustics in the hills of old Caroliny.

They can't hear the long rifles cracking and the hot lead thunking into tree trunks and bodies; they can't even hear Miss Pringle, who is saying,

"Here now, I want every one of you to lay a stone on Major Ferguson's grave . . ."

Some Big ENTRANCES and Doleful EXITS in the YEAR 1780 and ENVIRONS

KEOKUK, tragic chief of all the SACS, born on ROCK RIVER, now in the state of ILLINOIS.

Tough lucker JONATHAN CARVER checked out dead broke in LONDON, ENGLAND.

JOHN JAMES AUDUBON, bastard, first heard the birdies chirping in LES CAYES, island of HAITI.

Posthumous BLACKSTONE, Vinerian professor and author of the COMMENTARIES, passed from the scene in LONDON town.

JEAN AUGUSTE DOMINIQUE INGRES, prize pupil to DAVID, came in mewling at MONTAUBAN.

KARL VON CLAUSEWITZ, the happy Hun and author of *Hinterlassene Werke über Krieg und Kriegführung*, geb. in der nähe MAGDEBURG, DEUTSCHLAND.

EZEKIEL BISSELL, the Author's great, great grandfather, born in TORRINGFORD, CONNECTICUT, thereby assuring, well in advance, the publication of the present volume.

☞ SIXTEEN ☜

1781 rolled around.

It was now six years since Paul Revere lost his borrowed horse at Lexington.

The Continental Congress was busted and the War Debt was $24,057,157.

In April the Continental currency, which had been ailing for some time, died. Paper was being accepted at five hundred to one and lower.

In the North, West Point continued to thumb its nose and stick out its tongue at New York. Fun City responded by giving West Point the raspberry. But neither of them moved.

George Washington kept very busy shuttling around New Jersey to no purpose, and became obsessed with his spy system, concocting and leaking outlandish hoked-up military information designed to hoodwink Gen'l Clinton. Clinton was doing the same and as for the spies (some of whom were sultry Mata Hari types), they were working both sides of the street. This was America's first musical comedy and two ace tunesmiths named Bock and Harnick came up with a very snappy score.

In the South, American Generals Greene and Morgan were dancing around like water bugs. The main aim of their two lilliputian armies was to lead Cornwallis on a hare and hounds chase around the swamps and flooded rivers of this unlovely area and avoid conflict. They were constantly in motion, going ahead three squares, back ten squares, jumping rivers, like an Uncle Wiggily game.

General Daniel Morgan was forty-five years old and had rheumatism, sciatica and/or arthritis, take your pick, and his back was covered with scars from 500 lashes in the British army under Braddock. He was a very tough old party and not quite a gentleman.

Cornwallis detached bloody Tarleton who chased Morgan up country. Tarleton was so handsome he was almost pretty, but when on the war path he grew fangs, hair appeared on the palms of his hands and he was seen to slaver.

But Daniel Morgan was not afraid of the British Attila and took a stand to wait for him, at a place called The Cowpens in northernmost South Carolina.

It was a nervous night for the poor militia. "Tarleton! the Beast!" But Morgan spent the night encouraging the lads and going from camp fire to camp fire with words of cheer just like in a patriotic short feature called "Men Who Made Us Free" shown in the school gym.

The lines were formed in the cold dawn. The enemy was three miles away. The soldiers fidgeted in the cold and thought of home and mother and tried not to think of what was approaching.

Some of the King's finest were approaching.

The 17th Light Dragoons.

The 71st Highlanders.

The 33rd Foot.

The Royal Welsh Fusiliers.

Banastre Tarleton.

Morgan daringly put his militia in front, and since he knew they were going to run, not walk, to the nearest Exit he told them they could retreat if they would just stay long enough to fire three volleys.

Tarleton was actually a dummy whose only idea of tactics was the howling headlong charge. This time it didn't work.

Tarleton came on like thunder as usual with regimental band playing and British type victory cheers.

The militia fired thrice and retired in order behind the hill. Morgan's Continentals came forward and blasted the scarlet line. William Washington's cavalry came up from the rear and hit the British right flank. The militia had reformed behind the hill and now rushed forth and struck the left flank.

The redcoats threw down their guns and Tarleton,

Tarleton the Magnificent, ran away, and was chased for 28 miles by William Washington and a fourteen-year-old bugler who killed an enormous absconding hussar with his pistol.

General Morgan surveyed the field of victory and picked up a nine-year-old drummer boy and kissed him.

What do you and your bullterrier think of that, Gen'l Patton?

Everyone except Tarleton, Cornwallis and the yoyo British ministers was very elated over this affair.

Old Horace Walpole was still sounding off and he said, "America is once more not quite ready to be conquered, although every now and then we fancy it is. Tarleton is defeated, Cornwallis is checked and Arnold not sure of having betrayed his friends to much purpose."

Military experts and armchair warriors were soon babbling feverishly about this battle, calling it the most brilliant tactical operation ever fought on American soil and referring to it as "this American Cannae." The battle at Cannae, which he fought in 216 B.C., was the high water mark of Hannibal's career and considered technical perfection by connoisseurs of Armageddon.

Collecting battles, however, seems like a rather vulgar hobby to some, who would rather pop over to Wimbledon and watch the tennis.

Two weeks later the Continental Congress made up the "Articles of Confederation." As I write these words I am transported back to a school room in Dubuque, Iowa, in the year 1925. Motes of dust hang in the slanting flood of the afternoon sun, and the Regulator clock on the wall behind Miss Gussie Hagerty's head says it is five minutes after three. I am wondering if it will ever in the history of the world be four o'clock.

"Richard what can you tell us about the Articles of Confederation?"

The answer was nuthin much, and the answer remains the same today.

The hide and seek between General Greene and General Lord Earl Cornwallis continued until it became silly, and they agreed to produce a battle in order to keep the press quiet.

They met at Guilford Court House in North Carolina. It was another case of Bunker Hill pyrrhicism. Cornwallis won the fight but British gore was waist deep and Cornwallis lost nearly a third of his force and had scads of his best officers killed.

There is a nice Visitors Center here in 1975, where you can look at some more flintlock muskets in cases, and buy another imitation parchment replica of the Declaration of Independence. Two high school lads dressed in Continental Army costumes are giving a slide lecture to a sodality of Cub Scouts and doing a good job. They tell about the war and the significance of the battle and Cornwallis's over-extended position, all of which sails over the heads of the chubby cubs at an altitude of 100 feet.

Cornwallis got out of here in a hurry, so fast he left 70 wounded behind to the enemy. He hit the coast at Wilmington, North Carolina, where he took up residence in the Burgwin-Wright house at 224 Market Street. This is a beautiful layout, the admission is $1.00, and the lady who shows you through refers to the chairs as "cheers."

But Earl Cornwallis's number was up on the board, Kismet was calling, the Moving Finger was writing and he didn't know it but he had an appointment in Samara.

Ballad

Cornwallis led a country dance,
    The like was never seen, sir.
Much retrograde and much advance,
    And all with General Greene, sir.

Now hand in hand they circle round
    This ever-dancing pair, sir:
Their gentle movements soon confound
    The earl as they draw near, sir.

His music soon forgets to play —
    His feet can no more move, sir,
And all his bands now curse the day
    They jiggèd to our shore, sir.

Now Tories all, what can ye say?
    Come — is not this a griper,
That while your hopes are danced away,
    'Tis you must pay the piper?

        A Tin-Pan Alley Favorite of 1781

☞ SEVENTEEN ☜

1781!

Yorktown! YORKTOWN!

Breathes there an American with soul so anhydrous he has never spouted tears like a lawn sprinkler at hearing that glorious name? The grand scene played out here on the soil of the Old Dominion plucks at patriotic heart strings and makes them sound like a concert model Lyon and Healy harp. Cherishers of Our American Heritage put their cherishing equipment on overdrive at remembrance of Freedom's Finest Hour and proud Lieutenant General the Earl Cornwallis's ill-concealed chagrin, not to mention the petulant behavior in defeat of fiendish King George's arrogant warriors, beaten and crushed like beetles on a tap room floor.

O rare Continental Army! O grand militia who didn't run away for once! Glory to Knox, Lafayette, von Steuben, Hamilton and Washington! À votre santé most worthy Comte de Rochambeau! Let us doff our chapeaux to the valiant regiments of Royal Deux-Ponts, Soissonais, Saintonge, Agenois and Auxerre. Eternal grace on the head of your father, Rear Admiral Count François Joseph Paul de Grasse, and that goes for you too, Admiral Count de Barras, no matter how you pronounce your name. May the Bon Dieu de Batailles show his beaming face through eternity on the brave regiments of Agenais, Gatinais, and Touraine, and likewise on maréchal-de-camp the Marquis de Saint-Simon.

Long live France and His Majesty Louis the Sixteen. Vive les snails, icky livers of geese, et les inimitables pissoirs du beau Paris.

May, June and July of the Year of Decision were spent by Cornwallis in chasing General Lafayette all around Virginia. The Commander in Chief of the British in America, Sir Henry Clinton, spent these months in issuing orders and countercommands to Cornwallis which the latter used for gun wadding. From England at the same time both Generals were receiving swell advice, suggestions and orders from incompetent silly ass Lord Germain. (Germain was so haughty and obnoxious that even haughty and obnoxious Englishmen couldn't stand him.)

On August 14th, 1781, General Washington, to whom decisions didn't come easily, made up his mind to quit horsing around in New Jersey, New York and

Connecticut with General Rochambeau, and take their armies south. Ridding himself of his obsession with Clinton and Manhattan Island could not have been easy.

But Washington had received a billet-doux from the West Indies, from Admiral de Grasse, commander of the royal fleet of France, who had been teasing the British down there in the sugar islands.

De Grasse said he was bringing his big guns up to the Chesapeake along with 3200 French soldiers who had no use for Englishmen.

Washington put on his thinking cap. His genius machinery, which made sounds like a Newcomen engine, began to turn over. Presently a slip of paper emerged from his ear and on it were printed the words:

"Get down there you dummy. Cornwallis is on the Chesapeake."

Washington started south.

De Grasse started north.

Cornwallis dug in at Yorktown.

On the way down Washington stopped for several days at Mount Vernon. Washington had inherited Mount Vernon from his half brother Lawrence. The estate, or farm as G. W. always called it, was named for Admiral Vernon of the British navy, under whom Lawrence had served at Cartagena.

Washington doted on Mount Vernon with a passionate and very English love for the soil. Washing-

ton's English ancestry in Northamptonshire was aristocratic all the way back to Stonehenge.

Since leaving for Cambridge to take command in
1775 Washington had never been home. Six years.

While Washington was at Mount Vernon checking
out the espaliers and renewing acquaintance with his
hounds, the French fleet arrived at the mouth of the
Chesapeake. Five days later the British fleet showed
up. On September 5th, 1781, the two flotillas of cum-
bersome floating forts lined up off Cape Henry to per-
form one of those clumsy marine minuets of the time
called a naval battle. The discord lasted 2½ hours.

De Grasse, commanding from his flagship *Ville de
Paris*, a monstrous buoyant blob of timber and iron
carrying 110 guns, won the argument and in so doing
snatched the American colonies from the greedy grip
of perfidious Albion forever.

The two fleets drifted around within sight of each
other for four days. The British flagship *London*, 98
guns, had its masts in splinters. The British *Terrible*
sank.

The British fleet faded away in the direction of New
York, leaving Cornwallis to sweat it out.

Cornwallis was now in the bag.

The siege of British Yorktown by the Allied Armies
of republican protestant America and royalist catholic
France began on September 30th. On October 9th the
Allies began an incessant artillery fire which lasted

continuously until October 17th and could be heard all the way to St. James's Palace. All of the British batteries had now been put out of commission. "We could not fire a single gun," said Cornwallis, the ravager of Virginia.

A drummer boy in red mounted a parapet in the midst of the deafening bombardment and began to paradiddle for a parley. Nobody could hear his drum for the noise but all knew the meaning.

The guns of the glorious American Revolution grew silent before York.

An officer resembling David Niven appeared from the town threading his way through the trash of battle, stiff upper lippedly waving a white handkerchief.

Good Sportsmanship, an ingrained trait of English character (cf. "Playing Fields of Eton," "Captain Scott at the South Pole," etc.) was notably absent from the ceremonies of surrender that took place on the 19th of October.

General Lord Cornwallis, aide-de-camp to the King of England, Gentleman of the Bedchamber ditto, Governor of the Tower of London, complained of a migraine and failed to appear.

A great number of the prisoners were "in liquor."

The officers were all wearing new uniforms, not to give tone to the occasion, but so that said uniforms would not fall into the hands of the peasants who had through some inconceivable mistake beaten them.

". . . the British officers in general behaved like boys who had been whipped at school. Some bit their lips; some pouted; others cried."

A Frenchman was astonished and indignant:

"Throughout the whole *triste ceremonie* the English exhibited *morgue* (haughty arrogance) and not a little insolence. Above everything else they showed contempt for the Americans."

Proving that the Playing Fields of Eton don't have a chance against charming British self esteem.

There is such a beautiful innocence about Yorktown. The redoubts, abatis, and batteries all look — and it's so jolly to go down there to Yorktown — exactly like brother Ceddie's make believe battlefield, tin soldiers and lead artillery on the playroom carpet.

Such innocence and formality, everyone playing his part so well. Our Noble Commander. The great English lord — churlish to the end. Brave drummer boys, a stirring sea victory, regimental bands, and glorious banners waving in the sunshine of our triumph.

George Washington, moving like an institution, like 6 foot 2 inches of dolomite, accepts the unconditional surrender of an entire royal army on colonial soil.

The war was over and in two years a Peace would be signed.

The American People were at last free and they had life, liberty, and the pursuit of the dollar all to themselves, and the dollar brings eternal happiness wherever it goes.

Hundreds of years of peace, all with honor, would follow.

It was now perfectly clear that the American Dream would become a reality, and within 200 years the American People would be the Most Perfect Race on Earth, admired wholeheartedly around the world for perfect manners, modesty, and lovability.

With Leaders like unto Gods in their humility, integrity, and selflessness we face the golden dawn.

Well done, drummer boys! Well done, lads.

And flights of angels sing to thee in thy rest, George Washington! (1732–1799).

And don't look down.